Confronting Silence

Fallen Leaf Monographs on Contemporary Composers, 1

Toru Takemitsu with black cat. Photo by Daniel Schmid.

Toru Takemitsu

Confronting Silence

Selected Writings

Translated and edited by
Yoshiko Kakudo and Glenn Glasow

With a Foreword by Seiji Ozawa

Fallen Leaf Press   1995   Berkeley, California

Since this page cannot legibly accommodate all of the copyright notices, page 156 constitutes an extension of the copyright page.

Photo credits: frontispiece—Daniel Schmid (courtesy of the photographer); cover and plate 1 —Tetsuya Fukui (courtesy of Suntory Music Foundation); plate 4—Courtesy of Geijut-sushinchō-sha, Tokyo.

Library of Congress Cataloging-in-Publication Data

Takemitsu, Toru.
    [Literary works. English. Selections]
    Confronting silence: selected writings / Toru Takemitsu;
translated and edited by Yoshiko Kakudo and Glenn Glasow; with a
foreword by Seiji Ozawa.
       p.   cm. (Fallen Leaf monographs on contemporary composers, 1)
    Includes bibliographical references and index.
    ISBN 0-914913-31-X (alk. paper). — ISBN 0-914913-36-0 (pbk.: alk. paper)
    1. Music—History and criticism. I. Kakudo, Yoshiko.
II. Glasow, Glenn, 1924- . III. Title.
ML60.T258713 1995
780—dc20   95-9884
                                                  CIP
                                                  MN

∞ The paper used in this book meets the minimum requirements of the American National Standard for Information Services—Permanence of Paper for Printed Library Materials, ANSI Z39.48–1984.

Contents

List of Plates

Frontispiece: Toru Takemitsu with black cat

Foreword

I am very proud of my friend Toru Takemitsu. He is the first Japanese composer to write for a world audience and achieve international recognition. When I conducted the premiere performance of his *November Steps* for shakuhachi, biwa, and orchestra, commissioned by the New York Philharmonic, I encountered traditional Japanese music for the first time. In my training as a conductor I studied only Western music.

When I heard that Takemitsu-san's essays were to be published in English translation, I was filled with the hope that many new readers would experience the encounter with the writing of this remarkable composer of our time.

SEIJI OZAWA

Author's Preface

This volume presents the most extensive English translation of my writings up to this time. I would be less than honest if I said I am without fear and uncertainty. In addition, aware of the beauty and ambiguity of the Japanese language, I am concerned about how much of its nuance will remain in translation.

Despite the difficulties, the principal reason I write prose is to gain insight into myself. At the same time I want the audiences who hear my music to know why I chose composing Western music as my profession, and how I live and interpret this time in which I live. Certainly music may not need words. If one asks "is it true that music composition has nothing to do with words?" the answer is, "the opposite is true: yes, it does have to do with words."

To give clear shape to amorphous and irregular musical ideas and images, one cannot avoid depending on words. These are not the technical words of music theory but are instinctive, dramatic, communicative flashes. For that reason, at times words are for me a kind of filter of my thoughts, not the means of communicating events or emotions. In order to be totally immersed in music I cannot neglect verification of my relationship to the world through the use of words.

The pieces collected here cover a long period of time, vary in content, and are written in my peculiar Japanese. I appreciate the difficulties in translating them.

Fortunately my long-time friends Glenn Glasow and Yoshiko Kakudo, who have a deep understanding of Japanese culture, undertook the translation and editing. I cannot thank them enough. Also, I wish to extend deep appreciation to Ann Basart of Fallen Leaf Press, and to Mr. Seiji Ozawa, who wrote the foreword to these essays.

TORU TAKEMITSU

Translators' Preface

Japan has undergone recurring waves of foreign influence, which it has either rejected, accepted, or modified. Of these outside influences, the most dramatic occurred after 1945: the reorganization of the educational system, the change of attitude toward the imperial court, the intense Japanese interest in foreign things and ideas.

In this welter of changes, Toru Takemitsu appeared among postwar Japanese musicians, strongly influenced by Western traditions. Born in 1930, he graduated from Tokyo Keika High School in 1949. He has described himself as having "studied music composition under Yasuji Kiyose's guidance, but mainly self-taught."[1]

In 1951—together with performers, painters, poets, and several other composers—he organized the Experimental Workshop in Tokyo. In an account of the planning for its first exhibition, the group, at first provisionally named Group Atom, described its intentions:

> The purpose of having this exhibition is to combine the various art forms, reaching an organic combination that could not be realized within a gallery exhibition, and to create a new style of art with social relevance closely related to everyday life....

In addition to (1) "Painting," (2) "Objects," and (3) "Ballet," presentations would include:

> (4) Music: performances of the works in the exhibition space at fixed dates and hours and the playing of records of works by the members or new foreign music compositions.

> (5) Presentation of works as single pieces, or as a combination of paintings, objects and music compositions.

> In the exhibition and presentation above-mentioned, the entire exhibition space forms a [whole] in which the works are organically interrelated. They are not presented as single entities.

---

1. The brief biographical details in this preface were taken from *Toru Takemitsu: Index of His Works,* published by Schott Japan Co., Ltd., 1991. This listing includes works through May 31, 1991, appearing in the catalogues of Schott Japan Co., Ltd., Tokyo; Editions Salabert, Paris; and Universal Editions, AG, Vienna.

> Not every member approves the name of the group "Atom,"
> and Shūzō Takiguchi's suggestion [of] the name "Jikken Kōbō"or
> "Experimental Workshop" is adopted.[2]

This proclamation, with its interest in multimedia productions removed from the formalities of the traditional exhibit or concert, reflects contemporary foreign influences. A summary of performances in the group's first five years lists, along with local composers, the following: Olivier Messiaen (three concerts of his music), Béla Bartók, Norman Dello Joio, Erik Satie, Darius Milhaud, Arnold Schoenberg (a performance of *Pierrot Lunaire* [1922], presented a second time with staging), Aaron Copland, Leonard Bernstein, and Samuel Barber.[3]

These concerts suggest a preference for French and American composers. (Repeatedly in his later essays, Takemitsu expresses his admiration for Debussy and Messiaen.) This during the 1950s when Boulez reminded us "Schoenberg is Dead," when the age of Webern had been declared and European composers were concentrating on serial technique. In his 1960 essay "A Personal Approach," Takemitsu refers to the "dangerous aspects" of the twelve-tone technique with its "...mathematical and geometric pursuit of sound...." In the same essay he recognizes the possibility of noise as an element in composing. One may speculate about the influence of the Experimental Workshop on the musical development of Takemitsu, but the intense energy and dedication of its members was obvious.

The decade of the Experimental Workshop was important for Takemitsu as a composer. By 1960 he had received commissions from NHK and the Tokyo Symphony; won national prizes from the Japan Institute for Twentieth-Century Music and the Japan Art Festival; and received the *Prix Italia* in a competition sponsored by RAI, the Italian radio. Recordings of contemporary music festivals that included his compositions were

---

2. *Experimental Workshop: The 11th Exhibition [in] Homage to Shūzō Takiguchi*. Tokyo: Satani Gallery, 1991, p. 102. This 135-page exhibition catalogue of a retrospective show commemorating the fortieth anniversary of the founding of the Experimental Workshop included original photographs of the founding members, color reproductions of art works and manuscripts, and a history of its events from 1951 to 1957.

3. *Experimental Workshop*, pp. 104, 108, 114, and 124.

distributed by the Japan Information Service for worldwide broadcast. This, however, was only an anacrusis to a career that was to identify Toru Takemitsu as his country's most distinguished composer in the second half of the twentieth century.

Since 1960, Takemitsu's awards in international competitions have included two UNESCO Rostrum of Composers Prizes, the Inter Design Grand Prize, the *Prix International Maurice Ravel*, the Kyoto Music Grand Prize (a distinction shared with John Cage and Olivier Messiaen), and most recently (1994), the Grawemeyer Award. He has received commissions from the Koussevitsky Foundation and from the New York Philharmonic on its 125th anniversary.[4]

Takemitsu has been invited to international events: with John Cage to the East-West Center in Hawaii in 1964; to the Australian Canberra Festival in 1968; with Stravinsky, Karlheinz Stockhausen, and Jean-Claude Eloy to the International Contemporary Music Week in Paris in 1971; and to the Aldeburgh Festival as composer-in-residence in 1984. A composer without academic degrees who has never held a teaching position, he has two honorary Doctor of Music degrees and is an honorary member of both the American Academy and Institute of Arts and Letters and the French Ordre des Arts et des Lettres. He has given guest lectures at Harvard, Yale, Boston University, and the University of California at San Diego.

Takemitsu has always been concerned about Japanese music, traditional and contemporary, and its position in the greater international context. In 1973 he organized "Music Today," a series of annual concerts of international contemporary music performed in Tokyo's Seibu Theater. He served as music director of this series for twenty years. Japanese appreciation of Takemitsu's accomplishments has been reflected in a large number of national awards.

Outside Japan, only in recent years have concert audiences become aware of Toru Takemitsu's extensive work as a film composer. In the last

---

4. From the Schott catalogue cited on page xi. Again, these selected accomplishments in international music circles do not represent all of the composer's activities and commendations.

twenty-eight years he has composed music for more than ninety films, and has received twelve Mainichi Motion Picture Awards and two Japan Academy Awards for best film music. In 1987, his music for Akira Kurosawa's *Ran* received the Los Angeles Film Critics' Award. Takemitsu has discussed his attitude toward visual-music relationships in a recent documentary film, *Music for the Movies: Toru Takemitsu*, produced by Margaret Smilow, Yves Jeanneau, and Peter Grilli.

Internationally recognized as a major twentieth-century composer, Takemitsu as author is relatively unknown outside of Japan, largely because of the lack of translations. Since 1960 he has written essays and commentaries (most of them published in Japan), and some of his lectures have been transcribed for publication. These writings cover a wide range of subjects: arts, movies, his contemporaries, nature in all of its manifestations (a favorite topic), and, of course, music—traditional and contemporary, Eastern and Western, folk music, his own compositions and approach to composing.

The desire of this composer to express thoughts in prose as well as music—indeed, the importance of words in his own compositional technique (as he describes in "Dream and Number")—reminds us of nineteenth-century European composers and was not typical of Japanese composers before the second half of this century. Takemitsu, however, does not write program music, nor does he believe that words explain the essence of music. Although he is fascinated by words, amused by puns and homonyms, certainly writing is more than a casual hobby for him. Words stimulate his imagination and, in the literal sense of that word, give rise to images that in turn activate his sensibilities in his search for sounds, the essence of music.

The writings selected by Takemitsu for inclusion in this volume were written between 1960 and 1993. All have been published in Japanese newspapers and periodicals or as part of his collected essays. The grouping under general headings also follows the author's suggestion. We have borrowed the title *Confronting Silence* from an earlier collection of his essays.[5]

---

5. Toru Takemitsu. *Oto Chimmokuto hakariaeru hodoni* [*Sound: Confronting the Silence*]. Tokyo: Shinchōsha, 1971.

We have edited transcriptions of speeches at the Donald Keen Center at Columbia University and Studio 200 in Tokyo, to omit repeated comments and asides that seemed inappropriate for the published translation. In some technical descriptions, we have changed the author's identification of musical intervals to follow standard Western terminology. Japanese names appear in the order of given name / family name, following the practice of most Western translators, who long ago ceased referring to Bartók Béla.

Documentation presented problems. In some instances we could not determine the source of a quotation. (The problems that can arise in translating a translation are obvious.) Insofar as possible, we have tried to preserve the unaffected and poetic quality of the original Japanese. Special Japanese terms are translated and briefly defined at their first appearance in an essay, and brief definitions accompany entries in the index.

We especially wish to thank Nanako Ikefuji, President of Schott Japan, Inc., for her valuable advice and assistance. We are grateful for information provided by Peter Grilli and for the editorial assistance of Alden Jenks. The staff of the Music Library and the East Asiatic Library of the University of California at Berkeley were expecially helpful. We also appreciate the author's patience during the long preparation of this book.

YOSHIKO KAKUDO
GLENN GLASOW

Early Writings

Nature and Music

(from "A Composer's Diary")

— 1 —

This summer [1962], walking through the fields of Hokkaido, I could not help thinking that my own thoughts have come to resemble the sidewalks of a city: rigid and calculated. Standing there in a field with an uninterrupted view for forty kilometers, I thought that the city, because of its very nature, would some day be outmoded and abandoned as a passing phenomenon. The unnatural quality of city life results from an abnormal swelling of the nerve endings. In this way, though, seemingly active, hasn't it also become helpless?

A lifestyle out of balance with nature is frightening. As long as we live, we aspire to harmonize with nature. It is this harmony in which the arts originate and to which they will eventually return. Harmony, or balance, in this sense does not mean regulation or control by ready-made rules. It is beyond functionalism. I believe what we call "expression" in art is really discovery, by one's own mode, of something new in this world. There is something about this word "expression," however, that alienates me: no matter how dedicated to the truth we may be, in the end when we see that what we have produced is artificial, it is false. I have never doubted that the love of art is the love of unreality.

Facing the silence of the old trees I could not help thinking about my own work. My truth, however, is found only in the act of creation. And it is in that act that self-criticism arises and I feel alive. There is nothing profound about that.

Although I think constantly about the relationship of music to nature, for me music does not exist to describe natural scenery. While it is true that I am sometimes impressed by natural scenery devoid of human life, and that may motivate my own composing, at the same time I cannot forget the tawdry and seamy side of human existence. I cannot conceive of nature and human beings as opposing elements, but prefer to emphasize living harmoniously, which I like to call naturalness. To be sure, this contradicts fleeing to "the narrow road to the deep north." In my own creation naturalness is nothing but relating to reality. It is from the boiling pot of reality that art is born.

In Hokkaido I met some tourist Ainu who continue to wear their traditional garb—not by choice, but out of their own weariness from resisting outside forces. I also talked to some young white-shirted Ainu who looked down on the tourist Ainu. These young people held as an ideal the preservation of their culture in a pure state. They regarded the carved wooden bears and artificial crafts produced by the tourist Ainu as distortions of their culture. That may be true, but I was irritated and frustrated by the distance between the reality of the tourist Ainu and the ideals of those youths. Listening to their talk I despaired and felt like letting the whole Ainu culture die.

But there at the deserted lake, enchanted by the deep blue of the water, I could not forget those strong impressions that nearly caused me to lose my own identity: the Ainu woman crouching by the roadside with averted face, the shabby and somewhat smelly village. No, I do not underestimate the value of preserving a tradition. But those Ainu youths and I must remember one thing: as long as we live we must produce something. That is the natural thing to do.

I wish to free sounds from the trite rules of music, rules that are in turn stifled by formulas and calculations. I want to give sounds the freedom to breathe. Rather than on the ideology of self-expression, music should be based on a profound relationship to nature—sometimes gentle, sometimes harsh. When sounds are possessed by ideas instead of having their own identity, music suffers. This would be my basic rule, but it is only an idea and naturally I must develop a practical method. One way might be through an ethnological approach. There may be folk music with strength and beauty, but I cannot be completely honest in this kind of music. I want a more active relationship to the present. (Folk music in a "contemporary style" is nothing but a deception.)

Because the writer of popular tunes looks at his world with too much detachment, it falls to the composer to deal with the real thoughts and emotions of his time. In this welter of contemporary life it is only through his own sense of worth and by proving himself that a composer is able to relate to tradition in the most faithful sense.

— *2* —

I found Chikuhō had become an area of abandoned mines. An earlier vivid image of it as a place of bitter labor disputes was now replaced by the reality of abandoned miners' shacks standing pitifully weathering in the wind. An algae-laden crater lake and a tailings pile were only a pattern of deserted ruins. I stood there uneasily taking in the scenery as everything merged into a lyrical landscape. There were layers upon layers of heavy silence and I was beginning to feel that it was fruitless to resist it. I have never seen the ruins along the Nile River, but I wondered if those ruins and the scene I was facing shared the same qualities. I don't know. But it seems to me that for human beings, living is nothing but piling up the stones of ruins.

The story of Socrates rolling the stone to shut off the light of the sun is really the story of humankind. The true nature of history is something that could not be planned because it is only through living that a human being verifies his own life.

I can do nothing but walk on the track left by Socrates' stone. Everyone plods this fruitless road, treading out the path of history. This unfolding of humankind's history has nothing to do with fatalism or eternal principles.

There, confronting it, I resolved to face that silence as long as I can endure it. That is discipline.

Within our Western musical notation the silences (rests) tend to be placed with statistical considerations. But that method ignores the basic utterance of music. It really has nothing to do with music. Just as one cannot plan his life, neither can he plan music.

Music is either sound or silence. As long as I live I shall choose sound as something to confront a silence. That sound should be a single, strong sound.

I wonder if the task of the composer should not be that of presenting the basic unaltered form of music.

I would like to cut away the excess to be able to grasp the essential sound.

On the way back from a contemporary music festival I stopped at the Moss Garden in Kyoto. It appeared simple, but in its technical accomplishments I found it far removed from my taste. I do not like self-conscious artificiality. Even in composing, techniques are required to build up sounds and shape a piece of music. But even here, the appearance of effortlessness is considered an advanced technique. At the same time, a strikingly brilliant technique is not the mark of a master and is not to be admired. But this is all quite unnatural. The term "anti-virtuoso" appears to have a profound spiritual depth but in reality it is closely related to the intellect, and in the end it is really rooted in the notion of human superiority over nature. This is not the way to confront silence. We cannot avoid the silence of death that awaits us. For this reason I spoke earlier of the gentleness and cruelty of nature. If a work depends on technique it will be picked bare by nature, its bleaching bones left to become part of the landscape. Neither the edifice of history nor tradition readily reveal themselves. They are like the track left by Socrates's stone: invisible, delicate.

I wish to discard the concept of building sounds. In the world in which we live silence and unlimited sound exist. Painstakingly I wish to carve that sound with my own hands, finally to reach a single sound. And it should be as strong a sound as possible in its confrontation with silence.

— *3* —

October 6.... Heard *gagaku* [court music] at the Imperial Household Agency.

Certainly I was impressed by the ascending sounds that towered toward heaven like a tree. While the soundwaves of the music float through the air and by necessity exist in time, my impression of *gagaku* was that of a music that challenges measurable time. The Western method of capturing time in graphic form (using measured notation) and that of *gagaku* are completely different in their nature.

Gagaku lacks the concept of beat in Western terms. Of course, a certain rhythm is present, woven by specific percussion instruments—namely, *kakko, taiko*—and the *shō* [mouth organ]. However, they serve only to embroider the gossamer curtain of intricate sound. The symbols suggest a rhythm, but it is certainly far removed from the human pulse. As a pattern it is static. Occasionally it shoots sharply toward heaven like an arrow, as if to show the direction of the spirit. In this arena of sound even the basic primitive character of the instruments contributes to the creation of a mysterious harmony, resembling in this way nature's own workings.

There is even a sensual quality about the delicate intervals that resist being classified by the usual means. Heterophony is present like splashes in the stream of sounds, and yet it sounds appropriate.

The most important instrument here is the *shō*. My impression of ascending sounds and the secret of immeasurable metaphysical time seems to be based on the sound of this instrument. Sound on the *shō* is produced by inhaling and exhaling. The resultant sound, continuous and without attack, does not generate external beats, but awakens an internal latent rhythm. Delicately swaying clusters of sound reject the concept of everyday time. I now recall Pierre Reverdy saying, "Only silence is eternal."

Creating sound by inhaling and exhaling results in an unbroken continuity. While the pauses in a Noh drama possess a certain feeling of liveliness, the stream of sounds from a *shō* has an eternal repose about it. *Gagaku* reveals a strong Buddhist influence. In hearing the stream of sounds it is possible to imagine the concept of transitoriness but not necessarily that of lifelessness. Indeed, inhaling and exhaling are the history of life.

There is also something in the pauses in a Noh drama that has to do with eternity. Also, much of our traditional music aims at an immeasurable metaphysical sense of time. The unique qualities of this music would be lost if one began flirting with external form, but I need time to explore the real substance of that idea.

Western music has been carefully classified within a narrow system of sounds, and its presentation has been systematically notated. Rests within a score tend to be placed with mathematical compromises. Here the sound has lost its strength within the limitation of functionalism. Our task is to revive the basic power of sound. This can be done only by a new recognition of what sound really is. I do not know if *gagaku* satisfies that requirement, but I do know that in this stream of sounds that is *gagaku*, a richness of sound undivided by rigid classifications can be recognized.

I have referred to the "stream of sounds." This is not only an impressionistic description but a phrase intended to contrast with the usual method of construction in music—that of superimposing sounds one on another. This is not a matter of creating new space by merely dividing it, but it does pose a question: by admitting a new perception of space and giving it an active sense, is it not possible to discover a new unexpected, unexplored world? This is the same as recognizing sound as an object. Listening to the *shō* I began to think of a basic creative approach to negative space.

The external and internal world is full of vibration. Existing in this stream of infinite sound, I thought that it is my task to capture a single defined sound. The revival and reinstatement of *gagaku*, which has miraculously survived for such a long time, would be anachronistic in this modern world. And I myself have no particular desire to promote such a revival. I do, however, want to give serious thought to some of those things that *gagaku* suggests to contemporary music.

— *4* —

November 28. Will have a rehearsal for a concert of Ichiyanagi's works scheduled for the 30th. For the first time in my life I will be a performer. Seeing Ichiyanagi performing his own music in the Osaka Contemporary Music Festival I was impressed with the beauty of a human being so completely united with the sounds of his own music. And somehow I too wanted to become one with my own sounds. How wonderful it would be if the incomplete composer could be made whole by this act of performing his own music.

· · · · ·

In his book *Japanese Confections*, Jirō Tominaga wrote:

> I was surprised by the extremely fine craftsmanship evident in the meringue candy made by the master confectioner at Wakasaya in Kyoto. When I first saw the window display I did not think it was candy, but rather artificial cactus blossoms and bachelor buttons. It was only after it was pointed out by the master confectioner and I took a close look that I could believe they were actually candies. What kind of technique produced such candy? As much as I wanted to know, the process was not revealed to me.

I have had impressions similar to those of this author, but they are not limited to candy. Cooking frequently imitates forms from nature. But I think raw fish arranged in the form of a chrysanthemum appears somewhat comical and grotesque when one notices that it is really to be eaten. What is one to think of such elegance in food? Many excellent confections are made in Matsue as a result of the Lord Matsudaira Fumae, who was known for his discriminating taste. Judging from their names, such as "mountains," "river," or "spring grass," those candy creations must be beautifully made. Things like bean-jelly cakes are supposed to be served with green bamboo grass in harmony with the serving dishes. Sometimes the serving dish determines what will be served on it.

Matsudaira Fumae is said to have been accomplished at the tea ceremony. Concepts of *wabi* [cultivation of the serene] or *sabi* [tranquil resignation] provide one approach to contemplating nature. The approach of the West is different. I don't like the idea that everything can be explained logically, but I hesitate to discuss such philosophical matters superficially. It is just that a book about Japanese candy made me think.

Western confections have their own purely abstract forms and beauty. Japanese confections do not. As I mentioned, many of ours imitate natural forms. This difference is also applicable to many aspects of music. Japanese music, for example, seldom has purely instrumental works. In many cases instruments act merely as sentimental accompaniments to words; at other times they are used to depict the sense of the words. But generally in instrumental music, more importance is attached to appreciating the particular tone-quality of *koto* or *shamisen* [traditional string instruments], rather than to the combination of instrumental sounds.

Western performers are also sensitive to individual sounds, but these sounds are always part of a larger design and are significant only in their instrumental context and the framework of the piece. This concept, based on the idea of human beings conquering nature, is essentially different from the Japanese musical point of view. It must be said that in principle and construction, Western and Japanese music are fundamentally different, separated by a distance I find overwhelming. But the geographical distance between East and West diminishes daily and I must cope with it.

The Moss Garden in Kyoto was a disappointment, but the sounds created there impressed me deeply. Were those sounds originally a part of the plan by Musō Kokushi? The sharp sounds echoing from the corners of the garden were made simply by water running from bamboo spouts.

But the spatial arrangement and careful attention to the quality of the tone were not the result of mere skill. At the basis there was harmony: the harmonization of the sound—whether light or dark—with the shifting aspects of the natural landscape. Therein lies the clue to understanding the matter.

— 5 —

December 16. This morning I became a father. Mother and child doing well. Daughter was named Maki. Received congratulations from all my friends at the studio. Finished recording for the movie *Mitasareta Seikatsu* [*The Fulfilled Life*], directed by Susumu Hani. I am going to limit the scope of my own work. There are so many things I don't understand, even in a simple piano piece.

Met Tsubasa Asano from the Osaka Working People's Concerts. I have considerable reservations about the fact that this movement toward a new form began by accepting the form of the musical. It is strange that by some simple-minded equation this new so-called "synthesis" should be instantly linked to the musical. Rather than accepting the American-made musical shouldn't we look into our own *yose* [Japanese variety show] forms?

· · · · ·

In former times the Confucian ideas that music was ceremony held sway. Ceremony has to do with refined procedures, at the same time eschewing the direct expression of emotions. Without saying things directly one tries to tell about himself through allegorizing. Such an approach was regarded as dignified. The distance between the German *Ich-Romanen*[1] and the Japanese *shishōsetsu*[2] may also be seen between the Western music-as-expression and the traditional idea of music-as-ceremony. The bells of Westminster Abbey speak in terms of first person singular: they have an individual motive with a distinctive statement. The Japanese temple gong,

---

1. Novels based on authors' personal experiences; fictionalized autobiography.

2. A Japanese novel in which the author is the central figure; similar to the German *Ich-Romanen*.

however, speaks without personal identification: its sound seems to melt into the world beyond persons, static and sensual.

Yukio Mishima wrote:

> The Japanese language consists of sentences that easily eliminate the subject. *The Tale of Genji*, for example, has many passages where the subject is very obscure. In the case of the *shishōsetsu*, once the person "I" is established it can be understood by the reader without any problem. This is also true of "he." This simplifying technique, which includes the elimination of the third person and the mixing of "he" and "I," places the novel in the reader's own spiritual world at the expense of social and human relationships.

I wonder if the deep impression of the *shishōsetsu* might not be that of the beauty of denial of self. It impresses, not by confession, but by the restraint in denying one's self, which, while it limits and narrows the world, is at the same time emancipating. That is what creates the deep impression. Words are transformed into the fourth-dimensional passage between this world and the pure land of the future.

In all Japanese music I think *gidayū*[3] holds the strongest expression of violent emotions, although it is at the same time highly restrained in its use of the voice. There is no other example as vivid as this.

Does one express himself through his own suppression? Or is the reverse true? Either way a simple comparison of Japan and the West is meaningless.

I hope to define the characteristics of something Japanese, then, with those characteristics—personally confront something European of comparable value. At this point in my generation such confrontation of the two traditions should not be impossible. Whatever contradiction results may provide the basis for discussion.

— *6* —

Started a piano piece, *The Crossing*, in collaboration with the designer Kōhei Sugiura. It is through collaboration that I verify my own thoughts

---

3. Music of the *bunraku* and some kabuki plays; commonly employs one chanter and one *shamisen* player.

and reach out into a world of more complex sounds. I feel it would be ideal if my music could sound, and then when the echoes of those sounds come back I would no longer be there. I hesitate to sign my pieces these days. Should I leave them unsigned?

· · · · ·

Toshi Ichiyanagi expressed the following ideas:

> Result is a thing of the past. If you are concerned with results no vital action exists because the present is not known. Motivation and process are the important things. When a composer puts meaning into sound and invents fixed forms he objectifies himself through his own ego. Through his attitude one is removed from his own time quality. The Self is there without inventing it. And that entity of Self includes everything.
>
> It is not necessary to build fictitious reality.

I don't question the ideas expressed here; in fact, I rather agree with most of them. I wish to develop my "nature and music" by dealing with these matters in my own way. I must not ignore my doubts about the falseness of this so-called "expression"—they will never be resolved. But by confronting the imperfect act of expression a composer can turn it into a productive one. Could not the beginning of expression be the recognition of that part of one's self that cannot bear expressing? Expression is not the world giving meaning to me, but me giving meaning to the world. By doing so I reassure myself of my own existence in the world.

One does not regard the naming of the five fingers as expression. But grasping and pointing are expression. And fingers are part of the hand, and the hand is part of the arm, and the arm is part of something you call yourself. I can be only a hand. And that hand is certainly part of myself. The something that makes me alive could be myself. Just because I am only a hand doesn't mean we can say that my hand could not be a tree.

Expression never means separating myself from other things.

The world is immediately with me, but when I am aware of it, it retreats. Therefore, in talking to the world you are really only talking to yourself. Walk your own path, avoiding the influence of the senses, which often deceive you. It is only this path that will lead you to the richness of the world.

All art ends in artificiality; in that sense it is false. But what is it that gives it the ring of truth? I do not wish to make the invisible part of art fictitious.

Ichiyanagi says that when a composer puts meaning into sound he objectifies himself, but I don't think I really understand that. To me the world is sound. Sound penetrates me, linking me to the world. I give sounds active meaning. By doing this I am assured of being in the sounds, becoming one with them. To me this is the greatest reality. It is not that I shape anything, but rather that I desire to merge with the world.

— 7 —

I love collaborating. While I don't take individual efforts lightly, I am afraid that such efforts may tend to become self-centered without relationships beyond themselves. Establishment of the ego is a prerequisite for modern times. But to be fastidious in blocking out others would soon result in one's own death. There would be no circulation of air. Too often these days creativity is nothing but the invention of methods. When aesthetics becomes so sharp and distinguished, art becomes weak. Really, expression is nothing but the maximum realization and proving of self. If that is true I don't see that it makes sense to hold onto conventional techniques. I am afraid of attitudes lapsing into convenient routines.

As I have been saying, I am a composer whose thoughts are only the early glimmering of awareness of someone who regards composing as his profession. As a composer—not an inventor—I don't need patents. Things I think of must have been thought of by others already. That is why it is fitting that I be a composer, since I am not concerned about thinking thoughts that no one else might ever think. I just want to make sure that while I am thinking those thoughts that anyone might think, I am doing it in my very own way. Therefore, I think I don't mind if things are not always all my own.

Theoretically, the coexistence of two individualities is a contradiction. I am not trying to eliminate that contradiction by working in collaboration.

On the contrary, by experiencing stronger contradictions I hope to know reality. Is not the effort in reconciling differences the real exercise for life? Contradiction will result in movement, and that will make the air circulate.

> Hereupon, being is not being. Therefore, being is being.
> —Daisetsu Suzuki

Composition should be something that truly has being, something that should have arisen from the composer's own turbulent interaction with reality. For the composer, reality is nothing more than sounds. And for sounds to come into being they must reverberate through the composer, becoming one with him. The technique of constructing sounds through mathematical formulas is trivial. If music consisted only of inventing and constructing sounds I could well do without being a composer. If there is a sound that is alive, some kind of order will naturally exist. That is why we think the singing of birds is beautiful, truly beautiful.

The work of inventing and constructing music really holds no interest for me. I want to carve away the excess sound finally to grasp the essential single sound.

Joan Miró once said he would like to stop being Miró the Spanish painter. And Hans Arp participates in group sculpture. Might not this world of anonymous ideographic being that these people reached be a hidden source of reality? I finished one piece collaborating with Kōhei Sugiura. At many points in its composition we differed. But that is why the piece has an independent nature.

In that piece, entitled *Corona for Pianists*, the dividing line between Sugiura's work and mine is unclear. My contribution consisted of minimal, essential musical suggestions, while the spatial arrangement was Sugiura's. I was encouraged by the unpredictable events and discoveries. Many people, however, may be bewildered if they try to understand our work as an ordinary collaboration. Our work is really nothing but the smallest cell from which an anticipated organism is to grow. A certain botanist once said there is no formlessness in the cells that form bio-organisms. In that microcosmic world all cells follow strict laws.

Sometimes shapes like regular hexahedrons can be found. Amorphous shapes are found only in dead or injured tissue. Doesn't that tell us something?

— *8* —

Discouraged, I retreated into what resembled a cell in a beehive, sealed, without fresh air. No flags fluttered there. I had sold my soul for an easy system that had the superficial attraction of an insect specimen box. Actually, there were flags there, each on a straight pin, classifying the specimen and assigning it to its place in such a way that the desiccated specimen became even more real than the living creature. But it was a world without peace of mind.... I could not sing...no decay...no deterioration...time stood still.

A beautifully organized exterior without true substance!

But the stream of history flows on, carrying with it pollution as well as precious life.

Now that I have captured this concept of sound I must make it live rather than abstracting it into lifelessness. I must smash this glass specimen box, exposing my own fundamental error in pasting those classification labels on the realities of history. Never mind the shattering glass—my own wounds will mark the beginning of "life."

Circumstance and reality combine to shred my thinking. I must boil down this relationship to the point where "reality is nothing but sound to me." Reality is all around me offering the "tomorrow" I need to assure the promise of a future.

I have been trying to research the problem of the Japanese tradition in music. But I should be careful about making easy pilgrimages into the past.

Some time ago among the ruined mines of Chikuhō, I stood watching the frightening scenery in which nature reclaimed its own, bringing everything back into a sentimental landscape. Why was that so frightening to me? It was the fear of something man-made crumbling back into nature. Even an extremely well-crafted intellectual construction can crumble. Is it only geology that teaches us this?

To the human being nature is anonymous. Its scattered elements exist, potentially defined by their own names. True rapport between nature and human beings begins when we name things. It is then that the real exchange between things and man begins. When one sees a humanized tree, that tree truly exists. In other words, I strive to create an unnatural environment in my world. That is really a *natural* thing to do. For me, the naturalizing through allegory and metaphor that one finds in Japanese folk songs is completely *unnatural*. On numerous occasions I have written about the reconciliation of the Japanese people and nature. But now, by turning away from such thinking, I want to try to understand it in a new way.

What I have been saying is that we must give meaning to sound by returning it to its original state as a naked being. Sounds themselves, their movement as personalized beings—that is what we must discover and continue to discover anew. Organized sound is merely a subjective creation of the human being and is not the personalized sound I am discussing. My phrase "give meaning to sound" refers to something other than mere naming and differentiating. It concerns a total image. Both my acceptance and my suspicion of "chance music" stem from this point of view.

I want to carve away the excess to expose the single real existence. I must continue to work, striving always for precision and clarity.

— *9. Rich Silence* —

Saw the exhibition of Takiguchi's sketches. Descending the dimly lit steps of the gallery was like descending into the hold of a ship. A rich silence that sternly resisted any spoken sounds. In such moments—rare in one's experience—art withers if there is any attempt to embellish it with speech. This almost turbulent silence was dizzying. What kind of excitement is this? Words by Pierre Reverdy came to mind: "Only silence flows into the stream of eternal time."

Mr. Takiguchi wrote the following for his exhibition:

> I thought to fill a drafting pad with something other than characters. It wasn't clear to me whether I was writing or sketching. The indivisibility of the two is what engaged me.

The meaning of these lines is important and, I believe, very clear. Even without Reverdy's words, the excitement that seized me is something possible only with art. And those works—enveloped in silence, separated from the clamoring city only by a sheet of glass—made me think about the meaning of art.

The fear of silence is nothing new. Silence surrounds the dark world of death. Sometimes the silence of the vast universe hovers over us, enveloping us. There is the intense silence of birth, the quiet silence of one's return to the earth. Hasn't art been the human creature's rebellion against silence? Poetry and music were born when man first uttered a sound, resisting the silence. By scraping one object against another or by scouring a surface, pictorial art was born.

By the time of the Renaissance, art increasingly carried the taint of man. In the historical diversification of the arts, together with modern intellectualism, the very nature of art itself was threatened. In our time many of the arts have become exclusive and self-contained, each within its own narrow domain; no amount of verbal defense or theory will enrich such art.

Confronting silence by uttering a sound is nothing but verifying one's own existence. It is only that singling out of one's self from the cavern of silence that can really be called "singing." That is the only "truth" that should concern artists, otherwise we will never really face the question of art's reality. (Viewed this way, descriptive music is a cowardly art.) It is in silence that the artist singles out the truth to sing or sketch. And it is then that he realizes his truth exists prior to everything. This is the love of art, and at the same time is something that could be called "the world." These days too many arts have left the meaning of silence behind.

Incidentally, is there a contradiction in my reference to confronting silence with silence? I wish to be aware of the sound of silence in nature. Of course it is all right to replace this idea with words like "pause," referring in this instance to those areas of silence in the Noh drama, or with a word like "spatiality"—but the problems are more serious than the playing with terms or techniques. What is important is the way we recognize "sound."

In the past, music was built by piling up bricks of sound to erect edifices of varying styles. Today, of course, sounds can be reduced to wave forms, and one might say there is no difference between combining wave forms and piling up bricks. But sounds are the means to convey the movement of thought in the composer, directed at projecting a complex future image. If this is so, what we should be considering is those sounds themselves, the bricks of music.

In piling up bricks we build walls, creating division. Traffic through the doorways is symbolic, but should the arts be divided like that? Joan Miró once wrote:

> But truly becoming a man means getting away from your false self. In my case, it means no longer being Miró, that is to say, a Spanish painter belonging to a society that is limited by frontiers and social and bureaucratic conventions.
>
> In other words, you must move toward anonymity.[4]

What did art gain by dividing the space within those walls?

A door slams.... Let us imagine that I hear agony in that sound. But within the realm of physics, that sound is only a blue light glowing on the oscilloscope. We can reduce both sound and color to wave forms regardless of their own propensities. If this is so, was it foolish of me to hear agony in footsteps and pain in the screech of wheels? Physiologically and psychologically even those feelings can be analyzed, but those analyses show only a slight advance in graphic measurements beyond those of the oscilloscope, perhaps moving from the arithmetical to the mathematical. Such phenomenological facts do not offer a new way of recognizing "sound." Those facts are important to know, but if analysis exists only for its own sake, it is meaningless.

What was gained through the compartmentalization of the arts?

The words Takiguchi wrote to accompany his exhibition question this current state of affairs. Indeed, many of those sketches challenge that part of him that is the professional critic. Is not Takiguchi the poet, through the direct act of sketching, trying to recapture the Word that was one with God and was God?

Even without resorting to biblical justification we can say words must have life. But how is it today? Today many words are assigned the task

---

4. Joan Miró. *Joan Miró: Selected Writings and Interviews, ed. Margit Rowell.* Boston: G. K. Hall & Co., 1986, p. 252.

of naming and differentiating. Emaciated typefaces echo empty screeching sounds. Has our expanded vocabulary enriched anything else?

It is the keenly felt emptiness he finds in his relationship to words that becomes the starting point for Takiguchi's creation. In the "indivisibility of writing and sketching" he tries to grasp either poetry or pictorial art as an undivided entity. For him, sketching is a ritual by which the undivided matrix of the arts is revived. His own desk becomes an altar. Pelican ink replaces the ritual chicken blood. He crouches among piles of books. His incantation is silence. Suddenly he calls out, violently, with his own inner voice, summoning up himself like a spiritual medium. But this is not easy. There are always the unreliable senses one must be on guard against. But then...the white sheet of the sketchbook changes into an expansive stream...unbounded, mysterious. A sharp glass pen pricks incision-like marks. Pain...Takiguchi's own. He must endure it.

Takiguchi's work is obviously that of a poet because it is an act directed at discovering the original unpolished stone, rather than at polishing and presenting a finished form of some given material. Although it is very quiet, the process is something closer to action than to expression. Like oozing blood, the ink tends to create forms, unexpectedly ignoring Takiguchi's will. In this sudden reversal or that sudden reconciliation his own exercise in living goes on. It is interesting that those incision-like marks remind us of other forms. On close inspection the stainlike forms resemble human beings: some look violent, as if locked in the battle between the sexes; some are relaxed, like trees; original-shaped boats sail the expansive white river. As I looked I thought that whatever one's work is, if it is true, a human element will always be present. But we must remember all human efforts are after the original Creation. In their concentrated and directed movement of spirit Takiguchi's drawings are truly study sketches: an exercise in living.

My title for this essay, "Rich Silence," has two meanings. The first is synonymous with that quiet movement of Creation. The second refers to Takiguchi's quiet fulfillment in which the study for his future poetry is realized.

> In the beginning God created the heaven and the earth. And the earth was without form, and void; and darkness was upon the face of the deep. And the spirit of God moved upon the face of the waters.
>
> And God said, Let there be light: and there was light. And God saw the light, that it was good: and God divided the light from the darkness.
>
> And God called the light Day, and the darkness he called Night. And the evening and the morning were the first day.
>
> And God said, Let us make man in our image, after our likeness: and let them have dominion over the fish of the sea, and over the fowl of the air, and over the cattle, and over all the earth, and over every creeping thing that creepeth upon the earth.
>
> So God created man in his own image, in the image of God created he him; male and female created he them.[5]

A friend of mine once remarked that by the time he is twenty-five every man should have a port. Takiguchi must have felt reassurance in knowing that within himself he carries his own port, the waters of which reach out, flowing to the most distant shores. I had that feeling when viewing his exhibition.

In our modern society there are too many arts drifting aimlessly about, without a port.

— *10* —

A friend visited me, bringing with him his rough sketches—white space filled with notes, all bound by a rubber band. How do those sounds get packed into this boundless white expanse?

Moving my eyes from left to right, from top to bottom, I tried to take in the "life" that was coming into this world. The notes, scattered like constellations, seemed to glow faintly. There were interrelationships there, but they were the ordinary composed sounds—emaciated, burdened with function. It was all so familiar, this official graph: read left to right, from top to bottom.

My friend pounded out the ending for his work on my piano. When

---

5. The author has cited Genesis I: 1–5, 26–27, King James version of the Old Testament.

he remarked that he planned to conclude with that "sound" I noticed that the sound, which was not particularly distinguished, seemed to become something beyond itself simply by going through my friend's hands. The sound asserted itself by virtue of its own birth. Doesn't beauty exist by its own coming into being and disappearing?

Ichiyanagi began an essay with the comment, "The perception of nature in modern music is accomplished through the stop watch. We can no longer dream in the imaginary temporal world of 4/4 time, drinking in the sweet honey of sentiment." Certainly beauty does not arise from the lingering aesthetics of 4/4 time. But I wonder if one can conclude, in the words of Ichiyanagi, that "beauty cannot be born where it is sought."

I am sorry I cannot quote Ichiyanagi's essay in its entirety, but quite to my surprise I find myself wondering if his main argument is not based on the old idea of the unchanging nature of beauty.

As long as he lives, man waits for and longs for beauty. Even an impoverished society has its own beauty. There is beauty even in decay. It is also found in the quiet endurance of the fear of living. Many-faceted, beauty is the understanding of reality by each in his own way.

Why did the painter cut off his ear? Why did the deaf composer search for music? Since I cannot answer these questions I am not prepared to argue with the comment that "Beauty is not born where it is sought."

The sounds my friend pounded out were only the sounds of my piano, a little out of tune. To him it was part of his image, the complex features of which were reflected by my piano. He played badly, but I was impressed in a very special way because the sounds transcended the limitations of function.

I have another friend who is completely fascinated with the stains on things. Through various means he creates forms of stains that all look the same to me.

Why is he absorbed in such things?

— *11* —

There are several thousand Buddhas in the Nembutsuji Temple in Saga, Kyoto. Many of them are said to date from the Heian [794–1185] and

Kamakura [1185–1333] periods. The appearance of that line of stone images on a dark, drizzly day caught my imagination and would not let it go. Pelted by rain and weathered by the wind, the stone Buddhas are now reduced to simple stones.

From my earliest childhood I have loved stones. I especially like small shiny black pebbles, although I don't know what they are called. I like pure white ones too, but I think somehow the black ones have more weight and depth and look more like stones. Also, I like the sound of the word *ishi* [stone]. When I pronounce the word it is like spitting out sound and I feel all over again the strength of stone. I think the word *ishi* [stone] implies *ishi* [will].[6] Like Daruma turning to stone after facing the wall in meditation, stone endures. It does nothing but endure.

In the music for the documentary film *Nippon no Monyō* [*Japanese Patterns*], I used *biwa* [Japanese lute] for the first time.

In the West, the study of heraldry seems to be popular. Not much study has been devoted to Japanese crests. With no special knowledge about them, I am very curious about various patterns of crests, especially those having abstract geometric designs with rings combined with comma shapes. Their simplicity caught my interest with the same excitement I get from stones.

Designs that survived through centuries of history must have been drawn intuitively, but they seem ruled by some magical dynamics. Perhaps a world-view based on nature worship or magic produced those rings and comma shapes.

— *12* —

Some time ago, right after his *Nirvana Symphony* was published, the composer Toshirō Mayuzumi wrote an article about his profound attachment to the Buddhist temple gong. I expressed a kind of disapproval of what he had written because I could not bring myself to believe that the electronic analysis of a Buddhist gong was a prerequisite for the creation of that piece. Certainly the sound of a Buddhist gong might give a

---

6. The author is engaging in wordplay here. The phonetic sounds of the two words for "stone" and "will" are the same in Japanese, but the written characters are different.

composer some new ideas and techniques. I would not deny that. But there should be a great distance between the sound of a gong and the utterances of a composer.

I have no criticism of Mayuzumi's scientific analysis of the Buddhist gong and his attempt to reduce it to general musical terms. On the contrary, I approve. And his own subjective recreation of the gong sound is not the issue. If that were the case the problem would have been simple for me. What does concern me is the way Mayuzumi tried to explain that piece of music by means of the gong. I also had this feeling about *Samsara*, a recent work of Mayuzumi's in which the Buddhist idea of the transmigration of the soul is reduced to nothing but the role of a narrator, leaving me with the impression that the composer was imitating the idea with sounds. What is more, that simple explanation seems to be the basis of the general popularity of that piece. This is not intended as a criticism of the actual work. In fact, I have no doubt that at least the *Nirvana Symphony* is a masterpiece of symphonic literature.

In my opinion that gong effect in the *Nirvana Symphony* is not the most crucial part of the work. While Mayuzumi's article has a certain descriptive accuracy about it, there is something in the music that goes beyond the sound of the gong. That something is what I would call true expression, that special element that cannot be explained.

What was important was the way the sound of the gong, described by Mayuzumi as a "campanology effect," captured space and time beyond everyday life, shaping and moving according to the will of the composer. The actual gong sound ceased to be important. I believe that is the most honest approach a man can take toward the gong-nature, if one can presume to speak of the gong as having a nature. I feel the same way when Olivier Messiaen talks about bird songs, after he has pointed out that it is silly to transcribe nature in a slavish way.

> The words in poetry are something like iron filings on a sheet of paper: they can be arranged by a magnet and be made to rise, all pointing in one direction. Once a certain vital power penetrates words, the words themselves are abandoned, transformed by that power. Each word begins to show a magnetic character. Words gain direction.

The quotation above and the one that follows are from a study of poetics by Makoto Ōoka. I include them here because I think it is meaningful to think about the conditions he describes in terms of sounds. The excitement music provides goes beyond verbalization. And that is the reason we find meaning there.

> That time when we are truly impressed by a human being occurs when we see great power working within a small humble person. This is also true of words. That is, we are impressed, not by description, but by something elevated to "expression."

— *13* —

I think it is important, not only in words but also in my own music, to grasp the concrete sound that, in its confrontation of silence, should have strength and integrity.

While differences may exist between so-called spoken and written language, I do think that spoken words are stronger than written words. But this may be my own conviction as a composer. I have been using the term "utterance" to cover the physical and expressive sides of speech, and I have suggested that it is a symbol for "life." What does this term "utterance" really mean?

In the private quarters of the Rakanji Temple in Meguro I had a chance to hear some old *biwa* music. Hirata Kyokushū of the Chikuzen school of *biwa* playing once said to me, "Since my voice is low like that suited to *gidayū* it is not suited for the brilliant polished melodies of Chikuzen. Because of that personal problem I had to learn to sing from my heart much more than other singers."

What is it to "sing from the heart?" It was only after hearing a performance that I really discovered the significance of those casual remarks.

Generally it is rare to find individual invention within the singing of Japanese music. The music itself is highly polished and refined within the limitations handed down through generations. Technical experiments may appear but they too are restricted. In the performance of *jōruri* or other traditional styles we sometimes invoke the name of a specific virtuoso, as if seeking to reach his level of virtuosity. Why? Are we aspiring toward such divine singularity? If so, where is individuality in this traditional world of music? Of course technique is respected, but in this case respect has a significance far beyond the usual sense of the word.

There is a Japanese word, *iki*, which may mean "stylishness," "breath," or "to live."[7] A superb technique is not stylish [*iki*], not to be respected. On the other hand, virtuosity, which has the technique of making a long tradition live [*iki*], is respected as the superior one. That Chikuzen art is Hirata's own, but, paradoxically, at the same time it is not his. Most certainly it is Chikuzen. When the old melodies come alive through Hirata, is that not something beyond technique? That is what moves us.

Within the limiting, yet timeless, conventions of Japanese music, starting from the individual's breathing, it goes beyond the personal to merge with the pulse of "life," to become free. For me this has important implications.

Naturally the utterance of sound is not restricted to the voice. One has to have a direct physical relationship to the creation of that sound, otherwise wouldn't "singing from the heart" become a meaningless idea? Rigorous training is required for traditional Japanese music for a good reason, and it is not only for purposes of technique. Such training is really directed at uniting the musician's breathing with the immense "life" in nature.

As far as traditional Japanese music is concerned I am an outsider. But there are moments when I feel a sensual refinement in the old virtuoso arts, which goes beyond their being mere venerable masterpieces, a kind of distilled sensuality, something concrete. That is the quality we should not miss.

The quality I have been discussing is certainly utterance. At the same time it is something we might call a vision of life.

---

7. Again, from here to the end of this essay, Takemitsu is playing with homophones (in this case, *iki*) that appear so abundantly in the Japanese language.

From: *Oto Chinmoku to Hakariaeruhodoni* [*Sound: Confronting Silence*]. Tokyo: Shinchōsha, 1971.

On His Contemporaries

John Cage

John Cage's Music

John Cage profoundly influenced my music. Since he is constantly inventing new approaches to music, one cannot grasp the true nature of his music by looking at what is there. His musical invention, beyond any patent, is registered anonymously in the world. John Cage wishes to fertilize the barren "land of music." He faces that task with the humble soul of a farmer. To cultivate "the land of music," aren't human hands and feet still suitable? We are trying to get a large harvest from that inherited "land of music" without evaluating the soil. Generally speaking, that land could be said to be our traditional musical instruments. Without cultivating sound, no real originality will grow. Rules for music proliferate, but the question of sound remains obscure.

John Cage speaks of the "insides of sounds." This may seem like mysterious talk, but he is only suggesting that we include all kinds of vibrations in what we accept as a musical sound. We tend to grasp music within the confines of the smothering superficial conventions of composed music. In the midst of all this the naive and basic act of the human being, listening, has been forgotten. Music is something to be listened to, not explained. John Cage is trying to reconfirm the significance of this original act. For that reason it is impossible to analyze John Cage's amplified sounds by electronic means. *Listening* to his sounds is what John Cage's music really is. That is what any music is.

Genuine art always defies classification. Shallow and flimsy works are always measured by conventional criteria; they do not survive. The deep impression created by some art is not the result of the individual nature of the artist. Naturally, that cannot be eliminated entirely, but it is by our taking in the quiet revelation beyond the artist's individual nature that we are inspired anew each time we confront the art. Because that quiet revelation defies classification it is alive. It has various characteristics and it changes according to who takes it in.

The Quiet Revelation of John Cage

On one occasion the composer Pierre Schaeffer drew a suggestive diagram that clearly showed the idea behind *musique concrète*, the type of music he originated.

Abstract → Concrete
Concrete → Abstract

Conventional music expressed concrete images by means of abstract musical sounds. Conversely, *musique concrète* tried to express an abstract image by means of everyday concrete sounds. Musical sounds have always been musical by traditional definitions. Schaeffer's idea of *objet sonore* represented the final phase in the development of that tradition. As such, it needs no explanation.

What Schaeffer did was elevate noise to the same level as musical sounds, all according to classical aesthetics. Once again, music did not really revive. True, music survives, but simply enlarging the medium will not prevent the same old historical repetition.

Music will never become new simply by new sounds or by the enlargement of the medium. In the same way, a dialectical perception is only the methodical application of ideas. But the power that brings art alive is always beyond such personal consciousness. In the sense that contemporary aesthetics become more highly developed, the arts suffer.

When John Cage put nuts, bolts, erasers, and hairpins inside the piano, I don't think he was motivated by the same goals as Schaeffer. True, Cage did explore a considerable number of media for new sounds, but that was not the essential idea. If it had been only that, music would have gained nothing but freedom of expression, and it would have reached an even more unfortunate stage.

For John Cage, music is really his giving life to those things such as relationships, movement, dynamics—things that are called *music* and are within the framework of music but are really not living sound. That is why Cage's "freedom" has a bitterness about it when compared to that of Schaeffer. The connection between one sound and another may be compared to that between man and woman in that it takes place in so many different ways. In addition, it is a lifelike event, beyond aesthetics, without conclusion.

Since life is unnameable it defies classification. It is uncertain. So it is with John Cage's music which, as unspoken prophecy, allows people to react to it in different ways.

The World Is Full of Miracles

The forest was about thirty minutes on the highway from our hotel at the Kilauea volcano. It was a virgin forest, beyond the reach of human hands, full of wild birds.

The mountain weather changed quickly. By the time we reached our destination it was raining. The huge outline of the Hawaiian sun shone clearly through the steaming vapors and icy rain at the mouth of the volcano. The vermilion sun looked as if it were pasted on a gray wall. Then gradually it was covered with cloudlike felt.

The music festival in Honolulu was finished; John Cage and I visited the islands before returning home. There, in a forest full of wild birds, we could scarcely find the paths through thick ferns and bushes. Under the canopy of dark trees the flowering tropical orchids appeared to be from another world. I imagined I understood the language of the birds. Ever-changing things...bird songs never repeated...bright purple orchids ...rain...wind.

And then....

There in that forest I felt the things around me were not part of an objective world. I felt I was already part of those things. I was changing. If I leaned against a rotten tree I felt my skin would become brown, covered with villus. If I touched the leaves I would turn green.

With all the changes in the world, the world never changes. It is difficult to believe the unlimited manifestation of that Power that gives us life. The human being seeks to live by setting himself apart from others. Is this as it should be?

In Japanese we have the word *ikeru*, a colloquial form of *iku*. It has two meanings. One is "to place flowers in a vase to revive them." The other is "to bury a corpse." Isn't there something basic in this word? Isn't this combination of life and death a measure of the world? To Christ, who was executed on the hill of Golgotha, his death was a human experience. That is why there was a Resurrection. Was that a miracle? If so, the world is full of miracles.

Bashō wrote,

> As you look around
> There is nothing
> Which is not a flower.

This recognition is reinforced by Bashō's penetrating view of the world of nothingness, which is the world described as *ikashi* and *ikeru*, life and death. As you look around, that world is not the objective world. But it is there where subject and object merge. It is there that one truly lives. To place flowers in a vase (*ikeru*) is to see the world in those flowers and that vase. Unfortunately, even that act became formalized and tended to become representative. Still, the basic source of spirit is there. We could also call that a miracle.

As we walked through the forest, the trees and flowers constantly changed their appearance. John Cage was well informed about plants and about highly developed fungi. We found a bone-white mushroom looking like a stone growing beside an old tree trunk. Cage said, "This is probably as old as you are." The mushroom seemed to be the image of silence. We stared at it for some time. Why is he interested in things like mushrooms?

Cage said he goes out hunting mushrooms whenever he has free time. He said it is difficult to distinguish the poisonous varieties. One has to eat them to find out. In addition, some that are harmless when eaten raw become poisonous when cooked, and vice versa. He said it is quite mysterious. "Where does the poison come from, and where do you think it disappears to?"

It was when we visited Dr. Hisamatsu in Kansai that Cage said to this distinguished Zen scholar, "I have been concerned with the problem of notating music, but now I have doubts about putting my music down on paper." Dr. Hisamatsu replied, "Aren't you thinking that eyes and ears are different? We can hear with our eyes and look with our ears." Then he added that he thought the combination of both was more natural. Aren't we even forgetting how to see with our eyes?

Deep in the forest near a swamp, Cage found a rare mushroom. He said he wanted to take it to the museum near the crater because he could not recall a mention of it at the museum. We returned by car and left it there. He left a card with its botanical name. He signed it "John Cage." He also left detailed instructions for its safekeeping. The man in charge looked amazed and obviously annoyed. That was, in fact, the third mushroom Cage had delivered to the museum on that particular day. He said that mushroom was quite rare in the islands.

The world is full of miracles.

FROM: *OTO CHINMOKU TO HAKARIAERUHODONI* [*SOUND: CONFRONTING THE SILENCE*]. TOKYO: SHINCHŌSHA, 1971.

Merce Cunningham

Merce Cunningham is particularly beautiful at the moment of his disappearance from the stage. His disciplined body movement is not narrative, nor is it lyrical in terms of ballet. He has said that the lighting by Rauschenberg allowed for limitless physicalization of the spirit. One of his poses, momentarily frozen on my retina, never restricts my imagination. In fact, it frees my imagination. There is a saying, "At midnight the dawn is already there." Even from the darkened stage I received different feelings, as if I could see the dawn of the dance beginning to break.

The dance was conceived in such a way that no movement was ever interrupted at any point. Even beyond the final curtain that movement seemed to continue, gradually melting into the natural movements of everyday life. Merce Cunningham's dance shows a number of complex elements, including classical ballet forms and the subtle assumptions of mime. He especially loves clownlike Pierrot. Expressions such as laughing and crying alternated rapidly behind the screen of his own hands. "Strange Encounter" was like an elegant vaudeville scene. Cunningham recognizes such movements as originating in life. They may have been taken from the conventional stage, but they were revived as real-life gestures. Those derived movements and those he discovered himself became even more complex in their strange encounter.

My mother often tells me about the dances of Ruth St. Denis and Ted Shawn, which she saw when she was young. According to my mother, her impressions of that dancing were the same as those she received from a distinguished kabuki actor. Generally speaking, I cannot escape the feeling that the movements Merce Cunningham discovered in his dancing lean toward the East.

The slow movement of the dance shifts space into layers of soft gathers, like an aurora. It recalls the Noh drama where slow, nearly imperceptible, movement is used to express speed. The derived and discovered moments overlap. Space expands. And Merce Cunningham punched beautiful holes in that space.

When it was finished I was seized by a simple doubt: was the conventional stage suitable for such a performance? For example, the movement of a dancer running across the stage gets cut off abruptly by a velvet curtain at the stage wing. (This is not the curtain I mentioned earlier.) I do not like the black curtain of the Western theater. As a small boy it reminded me of the cloak that a Western witch with a crooked nose would wear.

Theater is something imaginary set within a limited space. If we accept terms such as "closed" or "open" space, the stage is certainly closed space. The world for which Merce Cunningham strives is beyond the capacity of that stage.

> What the dancers do is the most real of all the things we do. To pretend the man standing on the hill is expressing anything other than standing is simply "separation"—separation from life, separation from the sun rising and setting.... Dance is a "visible" act of life.

These beautiful words by Cunningham convey his ideas precisely. Isn't this the spirit of *haiku*?

I sat there imagining Cunningham tracing out beautiful movements in wide-open space.

FROM: *OTO CHINMOKU TO HAKARIAERUHODONI* [*SOUND: CONFRONTING THE SILENCE*]. TOKYO: SHINCHŌSHA, 1971.

Jasper Johns

Jasper Johns is a master of the controlled smile. He is an unusual kind of person for an American. He has light brown hair and gray Teutonic eyes that have not lost their meditative childlike quality. When we spoke he used archaic terms and phrases no longer in current use. It was confusing to me. This indirect communication gave him an air of gentleness and slight removal, but not enough to offend others. He explained that his manner of speech was effective in the troublesome social life of New York, but I had the feeling it was something more than a daily social necessity.

I was invited to a music festival in Honolulu, along with John Cage. Since I left Japan in late March, there was still plenty of time before the festival, so I decided to visit San Francisco to hear some concerts by David Tudor and John Cage. At these concerts I met many young composers I had known before only through their works. I also came to know Jasper Johns, who had accompanied John Cage from New York. His own retrospective show at the Jewish Museum [1964] had just closed and he was planning to vacation in Hawaii and Japan. During that time I had a chance to talk with this contemporary American artist.

In his James Bond-like, thin, black briefcase he carried a new deck of cards, a detective story, some filter cigarettes, and a sketchbook. His carrying such ordinary things left me with a strange impression.

During the trip whenever there was free time, he could be seen reading his detective story or playing Scrabble. Thinking back, I now realize the interesting connection between this Scrabble game and his painting. Single words made up of lettered white tiles were only symbols for everyday objects. But when they were assembled into more complex patterns, quite unexpected images emerged. What is the essential meaning of the word "red"? Then suddenly "arrow" would shoot across the board and the whole game would take on a metaphysical character.

In the plane from Honolulu he was reading John Dickson Carr when I heard the announcement that we were approaching Haneda. I asked him if he wasn't excited at returning to Japan after twelve years. "Certainly," he replied, without ever taking his eyes from the page where the guilty person was about to be revealed. He was completely absorbed in John Dickson Carr.

On arriving in Tokyo, Jasper Johns rented a studio and finished a piece called "Watchman," after spending nearly two months on it. The sketches for that piece that filled that sketchbook he carried in his black briefcase dated back two years.

I never heard him talk with passion about anything. He was always calm.

Jasper Johns thinks that in the relationship between society and painting everything other than the act of seeing is destructive. When the subject-matter of a painting forces its way to the fore, the act of looking becomes commonplace and restricted. As a first step in restoring the significance of the act, taking it back to its original simple state, Jasper Johns had to reject conventional clouded vision. Because his early works reduced the canvas to simple signs and images—flags, targets, letters, or numerals, for example—the non-pictorial ordinary quality of the subject matter reveals the artist's unspoiled eye. In these paintings he has restored the original significance to the act of seeing.

When Jasper Johns left Japan he left a work entitled "Watchman."

FROM: OTO CHINMOKU TO HAKARIAERUHODONI [SOUND: CONFRONTING THE SILENCE]. TOKYO: SHINCHŌSHA, 1971.

Conversation on Seeing

In his book *Défense et illustration de la musique dans le film*,[1] Henri Colpi, director of *Une aussi longue Absence*, says we should put to rest some myths about movie music. For example, there is that naive notion that movie music was invented to cover the hum of the projector in early silent films. But the early Théâtre Optique of Emile Reynaud already had piano accompaniment. And it could be pointed out that piano music was used with the Lumière brothers' cinematography in 1895. In short, the movie had accompanying music from its birth. Colpi says that music is, so to speak, a digestive aid for movie directors. He even goes as far as to say it is the music that determines the rhythm of the film. But there is still a prejudice that tells us the less noticeable the music, the better it is. This is foolish talk by people who are really incapable of seeing. The composer Hanns Eisler had a curt reply to such nonsense when he pointed out that if this were true, everything else in the production—the sound effects, direction, photography, acting, dialogue— might also improve if they were less noticeable.

I often think of movies in terms of problems in sound. But I think sound and words can be understood at the level of images because it is in the movie that these things, images-words-sounds, exist somewhere outside ordinary time.

I think that movie music has neither a fixed aesthetic nor an established theory. What I called the contrapuntal method used by Akira Kurosawa in *Norainu* and Julien Duvivier's use of the player piano in *Pepe le Moko* may appear to be methods, but they came out of the fixed idea that celluloid conveys only a story.

I remarked that sound is also an image, but then that is a remark by a composer asserting himself in the area of moviemaking. No matter what we composers do, it becomes associated with those visual images, and at the very least our sound comes under the control of the director. No matter how individual the composer's efforts, his sounds are directed and cut up according to a time element. I think, however, the better the movie the greater the number of contradictions. They are the contradictions of reality. As long as those contradictions exist—and they will be present because music has been added—I regard it as my duty to strengthen them.

One often hears it said of a movie that only the music was good. That is impossible: unless the movie is good, the music cannot be good.

---

1. Henri Colpi. *Défense et illustration de la musique dans le film*. Panoramique 1. Lyon: Société d'edition, de recherche et de documentation cinematographiques, 1963.

When I was a child, the strong impressions movies made on me came not from the story, but from the words and images, including the music. Put another way, they came from unexpected, altered reality. Movie scenes are constantly shifting. Movie music also must constantly change. But when I sit down alone to compose, personal feelings and immediate inclinations are inescapable. That is why participating in making a movie enriches my life as a composer.

Fine movies always present us with unexpected reality. The fascination in viewing a movie comes from its appearing to be a portrayal of reality; but it is not reality.

Some time ago when I saw Kenji Mizoguchi's *Yuki Fujin Ezu* [*Lady Snow's Portrait*], there was a scene with a mountain that appeared to me as a female form. Quite incidentally some years later I heard that Mizoguchi had begun that film after discovering that mountain with those particular contours. This marked the beginning of my more active interest in movies.

Isn't it true that from the moviemaker's standpoint there surely must be a recognition that "music is also an image"? In this same sense, when Jean-Luc Godard describes himself as "a painter with words," we get the feeling that he is grasping images themselves as words.

Primarily the composer should seek to attain the awareness of the commonality of music and words. Stated another way, for the composer self-realization is the writing of words in sound.

Take as an example the American artist Jasper Johns. In his group he is unique in that he has never made a film. When I asked him why, he replied that pictorial art is also words. I think he is right. Quite honestly, I think that in the many things written about "movies and words" or "music and words," no one has considered the problem seriously, and there can be no development if we simply understand "words" in their indicative meaning. Probably Godard is the single exception. In the movie *Une Femme mariée* [*A Married Woman*], there is a scene in which a woman goes to the airport to meet her husband. Not one word is spoken. There has never been a scene richer in "words." Simply stated, if spoken sounds serve only to develop a story, they are really not words at all.

And still we have no answer to this question of words and images, words and music.

In using words, whether in movies or in music, we draw closer to them. If you were to ask me for a definition of words, I would say that they are the symbols that arise during communication. But more than that, by using words one also becomes aware of others inside himself. Such things as "seeing" and "hearing" do not take place in isolation. They result only when another person enters you. It is then, looking deep inside, that you discover yourself.

Shooting Film vs. Seeing

Moviemaking is fated to capture reality only through the lens of a camera. For that reason the moviemaker does not have a clear awareness of this act of seeing or "peeking." In the final analysis it is this element that films are losing.

Peeking is one of the loneliest acts. But when you peek out and discover there ... another person—that is one of the dramatic moments in life.

We have plenty of moviemakers who "shoot film," but very few who "see." Very simply, I think from now on only those who "see" should be making films. As an act, seeing ranges from the naive to the metaphysical, but what is most important is the plain act of seeing. In moviemaking this peeking through the camera causes us to "see" a part of reality cut out from the whole. And it is in this cutting out that we discover the unexpected. Within the categories of "shooting film" and "seeing," it is possible that Julien Duvivier may belong in the first.

From now on there may be many ways of "seeing." I think Nagisa Ōshima is one of those fine directors who try to see. Recently, however, he seems to be consciously creating something to see. It is quite possible that "peeking" out to film and presenting the fixed images is not a healthy approach to moviemaking. For example, the films of Ōshima that follow that approach do not have the wholesome quality of his essays and political comments. Perhaps "wholesome" is not the right description, but Ōshima can "see." He "sees," for example, death in living reality. Without this kind of seeing his movie could never have been made.

Godard is also a filmmaker who naturally "sees." But occasionally I am nonplussed by his dogmatism, especially when, after presenting us with the intricacies of his own point of view, he ends by suggesting a single simple answer. There is a sequence in his *Une Femme mariée* in which a couple is driving back from a rendezvous at a hotel. As they talk and speed through a tunnel they mistakenly read the sign "danger" [*danger*] as "angel" [*ange*]. This is quite a simple technique of playing hide-and-seek with words. Godard regards words as images that are in the constant process of birth and death.

> Jean Cocteau once remarked that the movie exists to catch death as it happens. I think Godard begins with this point of view, pursuing his "seeing" to its absolute consequences. He certainly follows Cocteau in *Pierrot le fou*. In the end isn't our seeing really our feeling the constant "death" in that reality that can only be seen through the camera?

Indeed it is.

Up to now movies have been content to follow a theme using a standard technique in engaging the subject matter. But now, in the same spirit as that in the new movements in music and painting, moviemaking no longer follows fixed ideas. What is important is one's personal reaction to the reality presented. The movies by Susumu Hani and Hiroshi Teshigahara hold examples of unexpected accidental changes in what is being filmed. In this way these men constantly discover an evocative and exciting reality. And it is this reality that triggers the movement in which they turn their vision inward, to see deeply within themselves.

The Multi-Screen: Emancipator of the Montage

> Actually, don't we indulge in "peeking" in order to pique our imagination?

I really think so.

> If that is true, will the multi-projection techniques and the multi-screen that are so much under discussion these days kill the imaginative power of the audience?

I don't think so. While it is true that by multiple filming and projection something can be produced that nearly duplicates reality, it is interesting to note that it is not reality. The difference is extremely delicate, but that difference is the most important aspect of the movie. And it is here that we learn something: as viewers we can no longer relax and watch. We are forced visually into active participation.

To try to explain our interest in the multiple screen, I think we must go back to the original moviemaking technique. A simple multiplication of that technique into the multi-screen would be meaningless. But what is important is a basic idea in moviemaking: the idea of the montage. With present developments it may appear that all movies will soon use multi-projection, but I think the issue is not that simple. What these developments do is provide us with a point of departure from which we can begin to clarify the meaning of time in film.

In terms of the traditional montage, let us assume we have film shots A and B. In sequence, B always follows A. The montage was developed to make these events psychologically simultaneous. In multi-projection, however, these two scenes really coexist. Traditionally, the montage was an artificial creation of the director who sought to impose his own psychology on the viewer, but now, in multi-projection, it becomes possible for the audience itself to participate in creating the montage. So from now on filmmakers will have to re-evaluate the real nature of images, especially the time element in the film.

Up to this point the methodology has been trivial: B follows A. But now I sense a new spirit in film. As a consequence, if you are going to place B after A, there should be a new way to do it. After all, our understanding of these things is different now. In the early days somewhere between the beginning and end of a film there were sequences with unavoidable time lapses. To bridge these time gaps psychologically, the montage was developed. But now one can create a montage simply by using two films. Usually we do not discuss the multi-screen in terms of montage theory; but this whole idea is being pushed to its extreme point of development, and now would be an excellent time to change our whole concept of film.

Interest in multiple screens has been around for a long time, going back to Abel Gance's Polyvision, although his invention and current multi-projection techniques are fundamentally different in approach. I don't think the multiplication of screens necessarily provides the approach to new movies. We must remember that there is no other art form that is as sensitive to public demands and taste as the movie is. The audience demands larger screens; the movies change to meet that demand. Naturally, because the movie has long been commercialized, its ever-developing technology leans heavily on economics. But there are limits to this commercial concern, and we must begin to think about the very nature of the movie itself.

Now, having reached the point where even amateurs can easily make films, it is time for the professionals to concern themselves only with basic problems. What impresses us in seeing film is the originality, the thoughts and ideas of the filmmaker.

What the Private Film Should Be

The so-called private films have literally exploded in production and popularity in recent times. What possibilities do these films hold?

With all the recent talk about private films, can't we say that, in a real sense, all films are private?

Actually, peeking through that small lens is quite a private affair. Some films from small producers have been unexpectedly interesting. Humorous twists often result unconsciously from lack of facilities or skill. The dead seriousness of the bedroom scene becomes quite interesting when it is broken by something extremely funny popping up.

Generally speaking, I think wasting film is wonderful. We tend to be so thrifty, but it would be sad indeed if our seeing were restricted by the amount of film available. To really see, in the sense of movie seeing, requires much more film than would be used in actual seeing. It is wonderful to see that private films began by having nothing to do with the psychologisms or need for a story that drove the art of moviemaking into a dead end.

But I am critical of underground filmmakers in that I feel they should spend more time thinking about how their films are being shown. More people should see them. In terms of reaching the public, the film industry has a significant role. I think it was Chaplin who once remarked that money was the necessary addition to his own originality. Certainly it is a fact of life that an original idea, no matter how small at birth, will grow when nourished by money, the mother's milk of moviemaking.

Those thoughts that arise in "seeing," unembellished by anything like a story, may seem insignificant, but they have a distinctive basic power that is the heart of the movie. I am not opposed to the movie industry reflecting mass taste in order to attract a large audience. However, the fact remains: a good filmmaker cannot be found inside the industry. This is a strange situation that should concern us all.

The Complexities of Contemporary "Seeing"

There was a time, when Louis Lumière attended its birth, when the movie was something like a private film or home movie. Mechanical improvements followed. Then came the problem of popularizing this new invention, and finally the film industry developed. But maybe we should go back farther to ask, "What was the original concept of the film even before its birth at the time of Lumière and Edison?"

An interesting question. And that is exactly what I have been trying to get at. If there is an answer—and quite possibly there is not—it can be found only in the process of making a film. No filmmaker (and the same can be said of composers) begins work knowing what will happen. He works, asking himself, "What is a movie?" Others see his work and ask the same question.

The reality of something seen in a film, whether it be a Cadillac or something else, cannot produce another reality. By that I mean, in our production-oriented society, everything we use is being recycled. That old Cadillac is crushed and recycled. Curiously enough, we are fated to need junked cars to produce new ones. But the reality in a film stops there. It can produce nothing further. It is for that reason, as I mentioned earlier, that the filmmaker who truly sees, sees death. It is this vision of death that I feel in a good movie.

Moviemaking involves shooting film and editing. Quite simply, if someone films, there has to be something to film. There seem to be two ways to approach this "filming": one can see objects as parts of himself, or he can see them as being outside himself. There are people who recognize those elements as first-person singular, which is split into different images. It is impossible to say one approach is better than the other, but the point is, to start making a film it is necessary to see things. Of course, the eyes that see do change and are influenced. Recently the majority of filmmakers have been storytellers. And it is in this preoccupation with the story that the art of seeing things has been obscured.

An exception is Susumu Hani, a filmmaker who affirms his inner self through seeing the other world. The same can be said of Truffaut. This same sensibility is there in Godard, more complex and perhaps unfocused, but especially attuned to the new reality in America.

Jasper Johns has a series of works in which he reproduces such things as an American flag, a map, or an empty beer can in bronze. In his painting, because it is a two-dimensional art, he uses such things as letter symbols or maps. In these works we are confronted with things we have never thought of as being in a painting. Unexpected questions arise. These works usually become very active and complex. In a film, "things" tend to relate to one another without regard for what we expect, thereby deceiving us. I think this is the source of the ambiguities and complexities, and consequently the interest in a film.

The movie, at least as it is presently conceived, stands on a psychological time base. Even in actual daily life we experience time subjectively.

To avoid that, one would have to introduce a sense of timelessness, making a movie of extreme duration, viewing everything objectively from a fixed point, in the way Warhol films and edits. But when there is any movement in such a time sequence, people tend to follow it subjectively. Is time in a movie necessarily subjective?

At any rate, I have the feeling that our future movies will afford an unlimited variety of time experiences.

Beyond Criticism: The Origin of the Image

The Italian poet-director Pier Paolo Pasolini, director of *Hell of Apollon*, classified movies according to the techniques used. He referred to the traditional classic movie as "prosaic," to modern movies as "poetic."

> Classic movies are characterized by their "storytelling" qualities. The language here is prose. In contrast, the modern movie is characterized by its making the presence of the camera felt. In the great movies by Chaplin, Kenji Mizoguchi, and Bergman, in which poetic qualities are present, a fundamental principle applies: do not let the camera be felt. In terms of the "poetic movie" their works cannot be judged as image-oriented. Their poetic qualities arise from something other than the words as the expressive medium. The words in the poetic movie basically derive from a purely literary style.[2]

> Rather than the so-called "imageism" of contemporary films, I think this states the possibility that the camera technique, namely the subjective act of "seeing," is established as the "words" of the film.

Perhaps that is true. In the usual classic movie it was undesirable to permit the presence of the camera to intrude. But now I think it important to let the existence of the camera be known. I am aware of the camera when I see amateur-made underground films that, while not skillfully done from the technical standpoint, trigger a manner of perceiving that is different from the traditional manner. Occasionally in these third-rate films a reflector, a microphone, or some strange object suddenly appears. Such unexpected accidents do not disturb me.

There is the filmmaker who, very aware of his viewers, films objects for them to see. On the other hand, there is also the filmmaker who stands with his back to the viewer, he himself seeing. Image implies origin; but we must also not forget to consider the poetic or prosaic temperament. Those who are prosaic attempt to address the viewer through objects, while the poetic filmmaker turns his back to us viewers, so that it is as if we see the poet rather than what the poet sees. In the second instance the poet is there, but at the same time, he really is not, in that the viewer sees through him to the objects beyond. Very likely these ways of viewing the world are unconscious rather than deliberate.

Very few movies awaken consciousness. Most evoke a response in which the viewer identifies with the characters of the story, living the action with them. But we really need "films that awaken." In an interview

---

2. Pier Paolo Pasolini. "The Cinema of Poetry," in *Heretical Empiricism*, ed. by Louise K. Barnett, tr. by Ben Lawton and Louise K. Barnett (Bloomington: Indiana University Press, 1988), p. 183–184.

on the movie *Bonnie and Clyde* [*Oretachi ni Asu wa nai* in Japanese—literally, "There Will Be No Tomorrow"] in *Evergreen Review*, Arthur Penn discussed "awakening" at some length.[3] The cruel humor present there is certainly "awakening."

It was Cocteau who said that if one talks about "life," and is sincere, at the same time and to the same extent he also talks about death. If this is true, this is already something that goes beyond criticism. The very act of seeing is beyond criticism.

At any rate, one needs eyes to view the unknown. This is not the unknown so glibly referred to in science fiction movies. It is rather that which we discover alone, in a personal way, in our own special moments in life.

---

3. "Bonnie and Clyde: An Interview with Arthur Penn," *Evergreen Review*, no. 55 (June 1968), pp. 61–63.

FROM: *Oto Chinmoku to Hakariaeruhodoni* [*Sound: Confronting the Silence*]. Tokyo: Shinchōsha, 1971.

The Landscape of the Score

Hiroyuki Iwaki's essay, "The Landscape of the Music Score," serialized in *Tosho* magazine,[1] demonstrates the author's witty writing and observations as a practicing musician. It reveals the sharp senses of a conductor who tries to see beyond the reality of sound to the transitory landscape of the score. It is especially thought-provoking to me as a composer.

The composer's impatience and anxiety at having to base his music on a two-dimensional score, the insecurity at entrusting his own creation to a stranger (the performer)—such feelings are now understood as not being limited to the composer. Today's image of classical music is a narrow and self-satisfied one in which the division between composer and performer is not even questioned.

Iwaki's position as conductor is not that simple. Part of his role is that of a medium standing on the borderline between composer and performer. It is a position different from that of the translator, much different from that of the contractor viewing the architect's plans, in that the standards for interpreting the composer's score are not as precisely or objectively defined. One might add that music's real essence is protected by the ambiguities of writing. Grasped in the moment of performance, pitch, rhythm, even loudness are all relative. The notation of the score is a boundless symbol of the will toward precision, but it is not a recording of the results. The conductor's role as medium, and this may seem contradictory, is to grasp precisely that ambiguity and to express the desire for constant variety. That is, in a thousand performances he must reveal a thousand different expressions. It is this that gives music that special quality in which a single composition can be repeatedly performed.

Beethoven conducted by Walter or Furtwängler, Stravinsky by Ozawa or Iwaki—though using the same score these conductors clearly convey different musical results because they recognize those landscapes we call scores as parts of an ongoing unfolding of psychological event. (Incidentally, the precisely notated contemporary score or the economical score by J. S. Bach—which of these might be a model of our complex universe?)

In today's varied and omnipresent communications, the human ear has

---

1. Hiroyuki Iwaki. "Kifuhō no Gendaibyō: Gakufu no fūkei" ["Modern Malady in Notation: Landscape of the Score"]. *Tosho* [published by Iwanami Shoten] (May 1983), pp. 36–41.

been exposed to so much that it has become overloaded, fat, unable to bend to take in anything new. In the same way that reliable guidebooks guide the traveler, accepted judgments in music guide the listener. Even conductors choose the safe route. Many works we call "masterpieces" are delivered with unimaginative interpretations of the score—makeup on a corpse. Late last year I happened to hear the Sapporo Philharmonic's performance of Dvořák's "New World" Symphony conducted by Hiroyuki Iwaki. In this famous piece, probably known to every audience, every note so familiar, Iwaki discovered an unfamiliar landscape of sound never heard before.

I recalled that Iwaki had written a book on weight reduction for men, and it occurred to me that this "New World" of his was a symphony with a splendid physique without fat. The audience was surprised but performers following his conducting appeared even more so. I attended the rehearsals and could sense their bewilderment. In fact, I too was puzzled. But what Iwaki did was simply follow the score faithfully. He mentioned that he cut the fat from the established interpretation. The exaggerated gestures that resemble suggestive coquetry and have become associated with some works eventually appear to be part of the piece, and many listeners have come to accept them as such. Rather than taking what is actually in the score, even music specialists tend to accept or use as models the arbitrary expressions that famous conductors have recorded.

Iwaki explained that the "New World" that we generally hear includes over two hundred rubato passages not indicated in the score. In his performance with the Sapporo Symphony he ignored those conventional rubatos and faithfully followed the score as written. As a result I had the impression that the traditional sweetness was gone and the depths of the musical structure appeared. Moreover, the Bohemian sentiment was stronger. It may sound odd, but for the first time I realized why this piece by Dvořák is considered a masterpiece.

Maestro Furtwängler once remarked that for a composition there is only one interpretation, one way to perform the work. If so, was Iwaki's recent performance the only "correct" performance of the "New World" Symphony?

The answer is yes and no.

The measure of the "only performance" is the music each time it is heard, and that continues to be the measure for every performance.

Very likely for Hiroyuki Iwaki the "unknown" of music has become even more profound.

FROM: ONGAKU O YOBISAMASU MONO [SOMETHING THAT AWAKENS MUSIC]. TOKYO: SHINCHŌSHA, 1985.

East and West

On Music

A Single Sound

For several years I have been fascinated by traditional Japanese instruments such as the *biwa* and *shakuhachi*. After hearing some superb performances and meeting distinguished performers I wrote several pieces for these instruments. There was no other motivation, only pure musical interest and some curiosity. At first the sounds in this music offered fresh compositional material, but gradually they began to pose profound questions for me. Increasingly conscious of the sounds, I tried to re-create them, with negative results.

The sounds of such instruments are produced spontaneously in performance. They seem to resonate through the performer, then merge with nature to manifest themselves more as presence than as existence. In the process of their creation, theoretical thinking is destroyed. A single strum of the strings or even one pluck is too complex, too complete in itself to admit any theory. Between this complex sound—so strong that it can stand alone—and that point of intense silence preceding it, called *ma*, there is a metaphysical continuity that defies analysis. Like *itchō*[1] in Noh music, this *ma* and sound do not exist as a technically definable relationship. It is here that sound and silence confront each other, balancing each other in a relationship beyond any objective measurement.

In its complexity and its integrity this single sound can stand alone. To the sensitive Japanese listener who appreciates this refined sound, the unique idea of *ma*—the unsounded part of this experience—has at the same time a deep, powerful, and rich resonance that can stand up to the sound. In short, this *ma*, this powerful silence, is that which gives life to the sound and removes it from its position of primacy. So it is that sound, confronting the silence of *ma*, yields supremacy in the final expression. (Here I wish the term "expression" to be understood in its most general sense.) In performance, sound transcends the realm of the personal. Now we can see how the master *shakuhachi* player, striving in performance to re-create the sound of wind in a decaying bamboo grove, reveals the Japanese sound ideal: sound, in its ultimate expressiveness, being constantly refined, approaches the nothingness of that wind in the bamboo grove.

---

1. Recital of an excerpt from Noh drama, accompanied by a single percussion instrument, such as *ōtsuzumi*, *kotsuzumi*, or *taiko*; *itchō* displays percussion virtuosity.

What can I possibly add to that? Japanese traditional music is already a legacy to which no amount of reorganizing or defining will contribute a thing. It is equally foolish to make a fetish of traditional instruments. Such futile attempts contribute nothing vital to music. Are we left to believe that this traditional music has nothing to do with the contemporary musical experience?

In spite of all this, traditional Japanese music, like many other musical traditions in this world, captured and continues to hold my imagination.

Let us take two false notions current in musical thinking. The first confuses the act of composing with the solution of artificial technical problems. The second mistakes stylistic inventions in form for new musical values. It is to these ideas that the recognition that sound eventually returns to nothingness in nature rises to pose that ominous question beyond our own understanding. As a composer educated in Western music, it is there that I wish to walk... there, in that mysterious land where that recognition rules.

How will I take the first step? By cultivating within my own sensitivities those two different traditions of Japan and the West, then, by using them to develop different approaches to composition. I will keep the developing status of my work intact, not by resolving the contradiction between the two traditions, but by emphasizing the contradictions and confronting them. Unstable steps perhaps, but no matter how faltering they may be they will stop me from becoming a keeper of the tombs of tradition.

I wish to search out that single sound which is in itself so strong that it can confront silence. It is then that my own personal insignificance will cease to trouble me.

FROM: *OTO CHINMOKU TO HAKARIAERUHODONI* [*SOUND: CONFRONTING THE SILENCE*]. TOKYO: SHINCHŌSHA, 1971, PP. 196–197.

The Distance from Ud to Biwa

Because of World War II, the dislike of things Japanese continued for some time and was not easily wiped out. Indeed, I started out as a composer by denying any "Japaneseness." For someone who began by doubting traditional values, my first impression of Japanese music was unusually strong. The *gidayū* of the *bunraku*[1] theater that I happened to hear—especially the intensity of the melodies and the rhythm of the *futozao*[2]—made me aware of a completely different world of music. The world of sound created by the *futozao* was no less impressive than the world of the Western orchestra with its hundred different instruments. Perhaps to me it was even richer. Such comparisons may not make much sense, but my study of Western music only strengthened and verified the extraordinary emotional reaction I experienced.

If I may use a somewhat embarrassing term, the "human race" has many different types of music, including modern Western music, all of which influence one another to form the music of the entire human race. As societies and customs vary, so do their musical expressions. It is important to acknowledge this. Eventually there will be a universal music of the world's peoples, but that will take a long time, and the process of its development is not the issue here.

Many Japanese musical instruments usually referred to as native came from the Asian continent or the Korean peninsula. I am interested specifically in the *biwa* and *shakuhachi* and have written pieces for them. I am most interested in the Japanization of those instruments originating in China and the Middle East.

Musical instruments may be considered as extensions or enlargements of the human instrument. Or they may be seen as tools created to assist the expression of emotions beyond language. Viewed this way musical instruments definitely reflect the culture of a particular society—its customs, tastes, and the spirituality that society has nourished. Also, they must have been strongly influenced by the physical conditions of the people. Such influences show very gradual, nearly undetectable, changes over a

---

1. Japanese puppet theater.
2. Special *shamisen* used for *gidayū.*

long time, changes that are varied and difficult to discuss using a single example.

For example, in its shape the *biwa* does not differ greatly from the original Persian lute. It is said that the *biwa* came to Japan more than a thousand years ago, during the Asuka [552–645] and Tempyō [729–749] periods. When you think of such a long time-span, the external changes are slight, but the invisible internal changes have been great, nearly creating a different instrument. Specifically, those changes appeared in playing techniques, in the height of the frets, and in the different sounds that resulted. Until recently I rarely thought about those large plectra used by *biwa* performers. What necessitated such large beaters? No other instrument in the lute family requires such plectra.

The frets on the *biwa* are high and greatly reduced in number to only four or five. As a result the loosely stretched strings produce a considerable range of intervals between those frets. When we think in terms of other instruments such pitches are vague but impressive—hardly practical. But it is that vagueness that creates the special quality of the *biwa* sound. Strings stretched over highly raised frets are loose and free to vibrate. Finger movement is rather limited. Rather than being considered a limitation in complicated passage work, the important musical quality of the *biwa* is to be found in the delicate resonance of a single sound, in the shifting tensions and the resulting shades of sound. For such expression a large beater is appropriate. In the pursuit of the complexity of a single sound, the special notion of *sawari* was developed.[3] Considering that the shapes of the instruments are similar, the musical sound of the Arabian *ud*, Indian *vina*, or Chinese *p'ip'a* is much different from that of the *biwa*. I have an undying interest in this difference and in the Japanization of the *biwa*.

Today there are many Westerners who research and play Japanese instruments. My works for *biwa* and *shakuhachi* have been performed by Western musicians, and I have been surprised by the excellence of their performances. People may say this is to be expected. After all, Japanese play Western instruments, and modern Western music aims at universality

3. *Sawari* is discussed in detail on p. 64–65.

world of music. But great changes are underway among people, perhaps in the entire human race.

Recently there has been a tendency to play Japanese traditional instruments like Western instruments. This might induce changes in these instruments. But isn't there a need these days for us to take a little more care to affirm the indigenous character of instruments that have developed within a specific geographic area or ethnic group?

FROM: *ONGAKU O YOBISAMASU MONO* [*SOMETHING THAT AWAKENS MUSIC*]. TOKYO: SHINCHŌSHA, 1985.

Noh and Transience

"Noh," "*ma*"—simple single Japanese sounds for such complex ideas. We who use this language daily have tastes and customs different from other people's. Most of what people create or express does not exist apart from language or custom. I dislike generalizations such as "Western" or "Eastern," for even in such a simply constructed instrument as the flute one can hear subtle differences of a cultural nature in different geographic areas. Today, intermingling and swirling about us, varying currents from different cultures influence one another. Therefore, rather than the distant past, it becomes increasingly more important for us to understand our immediate past that supports these movements. Indeed, we are moving toward a universal language. But rather than unnaturally forcing the process—crowding Japanese sounds into Western musical structures, for example—we must recognize the varying sensibilities and aesthetics that give different cultures their special character.

On examination we find that the Japanese prefer an artistic expression close to nature while the Westerner treasures an artificial expression that is not part of nature. This is true of the Japanese preferences in sound. Historically Western music has striven to eliminate noise. On the periphery of Western music we find folk and tribal music, which creates unusual sounds that include noise. But again we find the Japanese seem to have a very special attitude toward natural sounds. Generally speaking, our performing arts came from the Asian continent and the Korean peninsula and were Japanized through the influence of Buddhism and other religious practices.

Characteristically this process did not develop such things as scales or rhythms but focused on the quality of individual instrumental sounds. This may be compared to the way the Japanese try to reveal the natural quality of a material while the Chinese apply extremely artificial craftsmanship to embroidery or sculpture.

In working with Japanese performers I often feel that they think discovering sounds more significant than expressing by sounds. While words like *ma* or *sawari* have actual technical meanings, at the same time they convey a metaphysical aesthetic. I think that as a people who developed the concept of "attaining Buddhahood in a single sound" (Ichion Jōbutsu), the Japanese found more meaning in listening to the innate quality of sound rather than in using sound as a means of expression. To them natural sound or noise was not a resource for personal expression but a reflection of the world. A performance of *Mugen* Noh, a type of Noh drama created by Zeami (1363–1443), in which the drama is concentrated in a single performer, is quite different from the modern Western drama that develops by means of the conflict between characters. Ostensibly the play *Izutsu* from *The Tales of Ise* is a love story about a beautiful woman and Narihira. As a main character the woman is called "the woman who waits" and is portrayed as the one who waits eternally for Narihira. (Incidentally, Paul Claudel wrote, "In drama something happens, but in Noh drama someone happens."[1]) In the second half of the play she appears wearing her lover's garment and becomes one with him. The depth of meaning here creates a beautiful sensual world. More interesting here is the situation in which a woman, a role played by a male actor, assumes a male role in the play. Rather than being a titillating question of sex this has an unreal aspect about it, different from modern dramatic Western situations. I find here a relationship to the Japanese language in which there is not first, second, or third person. And it all seems to stem from the Japanese attitude toward nature.

The master Noh player Hisao Kanze discussed this when I met him.

The question of how the Japanese relate all cultural matters to nature is significant. In Noh it is not a matter of people against nature. During the medieval period the adverb meaning "naturally" (now *shizen*) was originally the prefix *futo*—meaning "by chance" or "if you happen to." Thus, nature is not something that confronts humans but something one encounters by chance. Therefore, that must have influenced the experience of *ma* that exists between sounds.[2]

Kanze's comments left the strong impression that the impermanence that lies at the root of Japanese culture is not a matter of resignation but

---

1. Paul Claudel. *Claudel on the Theater*, edited by Jacques Petit and Jean-Pierre Kempf. Translated by Christine Trollope (University of Miami Press, 1972), p. 52.

2. The prefix referred to here was combined with verbs. Thus, the verbs *miru* (to see) and *omoidasu* (to remember) became *futomiru* (happen to see) and *futoomoidasu* (happen to remember).

of affirmation. It is the affirmation of life encountering a constantly changing nature. That encounter is accidental.

The distinctive Noh mask, different from the masks of any other country, may also have to do with this special understanding of nature. The Noh mask does not give character, but by covering the natural face that might show emotion, it creates in the actor an even purer internal expression. Hisao Kanze said, "To convey true expression we wear masks." Eliminating superficial acting places a greater demand on the inner element, which has a greater power to reveal things beyond the mask.

As the tree transmits to heaven the movement of earth and wind so does the Noh mask convey dreams that hover over the abyss of death.

FROM: *ONGAKU NO YOHAKU KARA* [*FROM THE MARGIN OF THE MUSIC*]. TOKYO: SHINCHŌSHA, 1980.

Sound of East, Sound of West

Transportable and Nontransportable Music

In our world there are human actions and individual emotions expressed through music that cannot be expressed by words. This sensitivity to sound, however, varies widely according to location and society. Naturally, with the development of transportation, an extensive cultural exchange also began. In the future varying cultures will be unified and, assisted by technology, eventually we will have a global culture. Until that time it is important for us to consider those peoples who have different thoughts and emotions. As a composer I think about music not as a mere recreation or pleasant pastime but as something that is part of a larger human experience.

The twentieth century is about to end. Significant in this century are the troubles brought on by modernization and the pessimism that developed along with technology. These things have ruled us all beyond our imagination. Now we are in the midst of a potential war crisis symbolized by nuclear weapons. Moreover, a distrust of things religious breeds a great pessimism, and feelings of powerlessness grip us. In such circumstances the great and immediate problem is survival.

In the face of these precarious conditions I began saying through my music, "Wait a minute—let's think!" Because of this, my music is not necessarily a joyous expression. Oh, I too listen to Madonna and Prince, perhaps enjoying them more than others.

I was born and raised in Japan where, though people have a life-style similar to that in the West, there is a completely different musical tradition. Of course the music the Japanese hear through radio and television is mainly European or American in style. But there are in this world strong, rich traditions of music much different from modern Western music—Chinese, Indonesian, and African music, for example. To really understand modern Western music I think it may be important for us to look at the music that is so different.

That simple term "East" covers a variety of differences. Although Chinese and Indian music have traditional instruments related to the Japanese *shamisen*, *koto*, *shakuhachi*, and *biwa*, the expressive character of these musics is completely different. Traditional Japanese music originally came from China and the Korean peninsula or through the Southern route, from India. There was no indigenous Japanese music, but what was imported from abroad was Japanized over a long time.

What differences are there between the sounds of the East and of the West? Naturally sound, regardless of its origin, can be considered as a physical phenomenon of wave lengths. In itself sound has no ethnicity. But when you consider the different places where people live and make sounds, or when different emotions are rendered as sounds, then you find that they vary considerably.

About 1,200 years ago, during the Tempyō [729–749] or Asuka [552–645] period, Chinese music was introduced into Japan. Over a long period of Japanization, one instrument, the *p'ip'a*, developed into something quite different from the original Chinese version. Many foreign instruments were to undergo such changes—such as the *shakuhachi*, also introduced from China.

I would like to relate an experience that impressed me deeply. In 1981 I traveled to a small island off the Australian coast, about 600 kilometers southeast of north Darwin. The trip took about two hours by light plane. To my amusement the island is called Groote, which means "large" in Dutch. As one of a group of eight persons of different ethnic backgrounds investigating the music of the Aborigines, I was the first Japanese ever to visit that island. Not even many white Australians had been there. About the time of our visit, a test excavation in search of manganese was underway. Some white supervisors were present. The island population of about 1,000 Aborigines is divided into two *moaeti*, groups of 500 each, living in the bush country. I stayed in a small shack, the home of an English missionary, and spent about ten days with the Aborigines. Island life was simple and poor beyond the imagination of anyone from a developed country. The island was full of wild oranges, papayas, and other fruits. There was a small stream. Early in the morning before dawn the people would go out to sea to fish. We ate those fish cooked in sea water. I had never before seen such a soil made red and black by minerals. Nearly all the Aborigines were barefoot.

Every day when the work was finished they would gather in a field to enjoy singing and dancing.

I was interested in that music, having read a book about the musical instruments of these people. There is an end-blown instrument made of a wooden tube that is called *didjeridu*. Rhythm is marked by striking a boomerang and a hunting spear together. The young people listen to the village elders retelling myths and "dream times"—accounts that survive from ancient times. Before visiting Groote Eylandt [island], I thought I was prepared with information on such things, but I realized how inadequate and inaccurate such book information can be. Of course we discovered wonderful dance and music, but the latter was far removed from what we would consider to be "music." In a way I was inclined to think that these people had no concept of music.

The song and dance of the Aborigines are connected with everyday life and are not developed separately. For example, people do not consider a musical instrument a tool the way we do, an extension of our hands or feet that we use to make sounds expressing emotions beyond words.

The *didjeridu* is made only of the wood of a mangrove or eucalyptus that has been hollowed by termites, creating a tube that produces the sound. In the Western sense this is not a musical instrument, something made and tuned by people. As a result the performer has to use an instrument longer than his own height. Obviously one person cannot carry such an instrument, so several people carry it on their shoulders. The sound made by blowing into this long hollow tube is as deep as the sound of the earth with a long mysterious decay. I was greatly shocked at the sound. In Western music, a tuning system called equal temperament was established about 400 years ago and has been widely accepted. Gradually instruments were modernized and made functional. In the process to achieve functionalism and convenience, however, important characteristics have been lost.

Even in European music there must have been subtle sounds or special regional sounds that the modern piano could not produce. But if one becomes preoccupied with such subtleties, instruments become less functional, so those considerations were dropped in favor of convenient standardization.

Of course it is not bad to make things convenient. That is an intelligent approach. But I was surprised to find a completely different kind of music on Groote Eylandt. It was not only there that I was so surprised. Some time ago I had a similar experience in the mountains of Indonesia, where

I heard local music in a number of villages. That music, however, was sophisticated and in a sense functional and well organized. So when I discovered among the Australian Aborigines a sound expression so much a part of everyday life that it could not be called "music" in the usual sense, I was astonished.

The sounds those Australian Aborigines created cannot be considered apart from nature, the land, or their hunting and fishing. Modern Western music can be taken from its place of origin and transported anywhere. I think it would be nearly impossible to take the music of Groote Eylandt from its own land.

It is very important for Western music to be disseminated, and to do this the frills must be eliminated. More recent technical developments have simplified and made it easier to disseminate music, but in the process that intangible, but most important element in music, to a large degree has been lost. Incidentally, it is to be expected that traditional music is very difficult to transport.

In 1967, nearly twenty years ago, I was asked to write something for the 125th anniversary concert of the New York Philharmonic. Several years prior to that I wrote a small piece for *biwa* and *shakuhachi* that Seiji Ozawa had a chance to hear. This great musician had never heard these instruments. Impressed, he took a tape recording of the piece back to the United States. Such a combination of *biwa* and *shakuhachi* had not been tried before, so my composition was a first attempt.

Leonard Bernstein heard the tape and asked me to write a piece in which those two instruments would be combined with an orchestra. I was young, had never been abroad, was happy with this request, and began composing. I came to realize that a fundamental, indescribable difference existed between Western and Japanese instruments. To some extent I knew that intellectually, and wished to overcome those differences and unite the two elements in my music, but it was not as simple as I thought. The more I looked at the two worlds of sound the greater the differences loomed, and I nearly decided the project was impossible. I thought of giving up but reconsidered. It became important to me to show an American audience the fundamental differences between modern European and traditional Japanese music. It might well be that as a composition it would fail, but I completed the work in order to show as great a difference between the two traditions as possible without blending them.

It was performed in November, and to me that project represented a new step: thus, I titled the work *November Steps*. In Japanese music, *danmono* are the equivalent of Western variations, and the word *dan* means step. My "November Steps" are a set of eleven variations.

Unlike Tokyo, New York City in November was extremely dry. Because of that one of the *shakuhachi* left in the hotel room split. The *biwa* was also affected; to the performers' bewilderment, its strings became very tight. The performers sprinkled water on the hotel room floor, wrapped their instruments in wet gauze, even bought lettuce leaves with which to wrap the instruments. These were simply physical conditions, but we certainly felt the difficulties in exporting Japanese music. On the contrary, European instruments brought to Japan have little difficulty because of the humidity. Of course a piano may go out of tune but comparatively speaking there would be no problems as severe as those we had with the *biwa* and *shakuhachi*. European instruments are made to be adaptable.

Because of that experience I regarded Japanese instruments as very limited, but I began wondering what those limitations might mean to art. Among Japanese instruments I know most about the *biwa* and *shakuhachi* and tend to refer to them often, but the same comments could be applied to the *koto* and *shamisen*. Gradually I came to realize that the shortcomings I saw in the *biwa* and *shakuhachi* are at the same time very important elements in Japanese music.

Passing through India it was called the *vina*, in China the *p'ip'a*, in Japan the *biwa*. The *vina* and *p'ip'a* are closer to European instruments and are made for easier performance; they are designed to play more precise intervals. Like the guitar, the *p'ip'a* has a large number of frets; by pressing the string against a fret the performer produces a fixed pitch. For some unknown reason there are fewer frets on the *biwa*, and the strings are stretched more loosely. On the *biwa* the different pitches result from stopping these loose strings between the frets. Accordingly, three to four different pitches can be produced between two frets. Frets exist to make precise and predictable pitches possible but the Japanese *biwa* ignores that.

As a result, the *biwa* is not predictable. Fast passages are nearly impossible, and performances tend to emphasize subtle variation and decay in sounds.

It is not clear why those changes occurred in the instrument. I suspect there may be religious reasons, climatic conditions, or some such influences that are not purely musical.

Similar things could be said of the *shakuhachi*. Its sound, if you try to describe it, is dark and desolate. But the sound of the traditional Chinese flute is light and bright. After the instrument's arrival in Japan, a peculiar *shakuhachi* quality developed with its ambiguous split pitches made by pressing the finger holes and using different fingerings.

Tradition of Sawari

The *biwa* could be called the mother of Japanese music. The major characteristic that sets it apart from Western instruments in the active inclusion of noise in its sound, whereas Western instruments, in the process of development, sought to eliminate noise. It may sound contradictory to refer to "beautiful noise," but the *biwa* is constructed to create such a sound. That sound is called *sawari*, a term that also has come to be used in a general sense, as we will see.

On the *biwa* the *sawari* is part of the neck of the instrument where four or five strings are stretched over a grooved ivory plate. When a string is stretched between these grooves and plucked, it strikes the grooves and makes a noise. The concave area of this ivory plate is called the "valley of the *sawari*," the convex area the "mountain of the *sawari*," and the entire plate simply *sawari*. When a string is stretched between these grooves and plucked, it strikes the grooves and makes a noisy "bin."

The term *sawari* may also mean "to touch." But this term, more than referring to a part of an instrument or touching, contains a much wider significance useful in understanding Japanese aesthetics.

In a book from the Edo period [1615–1867], the *biwa* player is advised to try to imitate the sound of the cicada. The *biwa* is deliberately designed, with *sawari* plate, to create such insect sounds. This is also true of the *shamisen*.

The term *sawari*, which also means "touch," may additionally mean "obstacle." Thus, *sawari* is the "apparatus of an obstacle" itself. In a sense it is an intentional inconvenience that creates a part of the expressiveness of the sound. Compared to the Western attitude toward musical instruments, this deliberate obstruction represents a very different approach to sound.

In the kabuki repertory there are many long works such as *Chūshingura*. When one sees only the famous scenes this is referred to as "viewing only the *sawari*." In this sense *sawari* is a very important part of a work.

What we call *hōgaku* today is that collection of traditional pieces developed and refined by the Edo population. Why did those people bring *sawari* (understood now in the sense of obstacles) into their music? Whether the reasons were political, religious, or social is not clear to me.

The monthly biological function in women is also referred to in Japanese as the "monthly *sawari*"—a natural inconvenience for women but essential for producing children. For me there is something symbolic about this: the inconvenience is potentially creative. In music the artificial inconvenience in creating sound produces the sound. The resulting *biwa* sound is strong, ambiguous, deeply significant. While the Japanese *biwa* cannot execute the fast passages that are part of the Chinese *p'ip'a* technique, it is capable of complex, profound, and wonderful sounds.

We can see that the Japanese and Western approaches to music are quite different. We speak of essential elements in Western music—rhythm, melody, and harmony. Japanese music considers the quality of sound rather than melody. The inclusion in music of a natural noise, such as the sound of the cicada, symbolizes the development of the Japanese appreciation of complex sounds.

Of *shakuhachi* music it is often said, "Ichion Jōbutsu"—"With one sound one becomes the Buddha"—suggesting that the universe is explored in a single sound. This may be a characteristic Buddhist feeling but it is not necessarily only Buddhism that influences Japanese sensibilities.

Following World War II, I studied Western music, at the same time thinking about myself and the time in which I lived. In the process, quite by chance, I came to know traditional Japanese music and, as a result, other Asian musical traditions. I came to realize that a large part of the world's music is quite different from that of the West.

Western modernism is directed at functionalism and convenience, and the Japanese are an extreme example of people pursuing these goals and enjoying the results. But there are many kinds of music on this earth—Australian Aboriginal and traditional Japanese are examples—that seek utmost freedom within their own traditional limitations.

The unique style in the Japanese Noh drama has attracted attention in Europe and the United States. The number of foreigners studying Noh in Japan is increasing and Noh players have performed abroad in Paris and New York.

The *nohkan*, the flute used in the Noh ensemble, was originally called *ryūteki* and was used in *gagaku* [old Japanese court music]. This was also originally a Chinese instrument but the Noh players changed it by means of a tongue-like addition to the bamboo tube, intentionally altering its sound.

This unique sound of the *nohkan* is also an example of *sawari*—a Japanization in which sound is intentionally obstructed, a notion of sound quite different from that in the West. So, with some exaggeration, I might say God dwells in a single sound.

A single sound, say *do* in the scale, has no particular meaning. But if we follow it with another pitch, then another, the Western dialectic of sound association begins. In such an association of sounds, the Western notion of musical expression is born. In this music the individual sound elements have less individual meaning as they function to create the artistic expression. If they had varied individual meanings, they would be less functional in contributing to the total expression. Modern European music is most concerned with synthesizing and organizing sound to create a unique expression. Such thinking led to the creation of today's synthesizer.

Didn't sound exist in old Europe as an undifferentiated mass of sound? But by dividing pitches into semitones, then into smaller divisions, didn't we finally reach sounds that are not part of the harmonic overtone series? By using such unnatural, uncharacteristic sounds and by mixing sounds, using synthesizers and computers, we create different new sounds. At the opposite end of the spectrum from these artificially created sounds are the sounds of the *biwa, shakuhachi,* and the Australian *didjeridu.* It is these two extremes that I have called the "sound of the East, sound of the West," or "portable and nonportable sound." But I think we must look very carefully at both of these traditions.

I live in today's society, with the same life-style as Westerners, and daily am in touch with political, economic, social, and artistic events in the world. I am not in the Edo period but in the closing years of the twentieth century. I happen to have been born in Japan of Japanese parents and grew up in Japan. Shortly after the war, I studied Western music; after ten years I discovered Japanese traditional music, which confused me. At the same time I was charmed by its beauty. However, I was not able to plunge into it uncritically, perhaps because of my study and knowledge of Western music, but also because I live in modern times. I have been trying not to view Japan as an absolute but as a duality, otherwise the tradition does not come alive but remains a meaningless antique. When I composed for *shakuhachi* and *biwa* it was an unavoidable education for me. I was experiencing a European revolution and a Japanese tradition. But now, as we incubate this universal cosmic egg, that may no longer be such a special experience. We have to wait for that egg to hatch, recognizing various cultures with as many possible approaches and with as much time as needed.

November Steps attracted great attention. Many young composers came to notice things Japanese. At that time I felt quite ambivalent. Today's young people do not share that ambivalence. Perhaps they have no sense of crisis; in fact, they handle two different traditions skillfully. In the near future there may appear a new culture with a new universal scope, but it will take time and, as I mentioned earlier, we should take our time. Too rapid a change may result in something lopsided.

Composing *November Steps* was an invaluable experience for me. I realized the wide expanse of music and gained the great hope that humanity can come to understand our different cultures.

THIS IS AN EDITED VERSION OF THE TRANSCRIPT OF A LECTURE DELIVERED IN NOVEMBER 1989 AT THE DONALD KEEN CENTER AT COLUMBIA UNIVERSITY. IT WAS ORIGINALLY PUBLISHED IN JAPAN UNDER THE TITLE *SOUND OF EAST, SOUND OF WEST: ABOUT THE CULTURE OF SAWARI*. FROM: "HIGASHI NO OTO, NISHI NO OTO. SAWARI NO BUNKA NI TSUITE," *MONTHLY SHINCHŌ*, TOKYO: SHINCHŌSHA (JAN. 1990).

On Art

Isamu Noguchi —Traveler

In his preface to Isamu Noguchi's *A Sculptor's World*,[1] Buckminster Fuller pointed out that because of the invention of the airplane the historical accomplishments of different, previously isolated nations now approach an historical and geographic merger. Noguchi was born in the early twentieth century, about the time the airplane was invented; and we find Fuller making frequent use of the word "travel" in his evocative allusions to Noguchi's life and work. Long before I read that preface my admiration for Noguchi's works was embellished by the thoughts of travel they evoked, an unintellectual, emotional response. But it was Fuller's intuitive powers expressed through his words that made that response clearer to me.

Noguchi is a traveler. My acquaintance with him and the experience of seeing his works ended my comfortable existence and set me on the path to the world of the unknown. But what Noguchi brings back from his travels takes different forms, some sculptural, sometimes unfinished garden designs, but always something that enriches me and makes me aware of new places on my own map.

Travel, usually understood as movement toward a temporary destination, is really an unlimited process beyond action. Therefore, true travel is endless. When we choose to remain at one destination the act of expression is controlled by established beauty: travel has become meaningless. But traveling as Noguchi does is not easy.

Within the limitless reverberations of his works I experience a single constant tension. That is, his work does not end with the completion of a single piece but goes on in an unending pursuit of the true nature of an object and of life. These works are not end results but are the expression of an unrestrainable desire for eternity, filled with beginning anticipation. To me they are very sensual works. Convex forms, for example, often have lines like a living body in which carved cavities seem to appear like dark abysses. Perhaps such things express a fundamental sensuality to me.

Noguchi intensely dislikes works that cleverly reorganize past art. His strong interest in the techniques and spiritual values of different cultures nourished by past nations is rooted in his realization that "sculptures are transfigurations, magical distillations," and are not merely a special class of beautiful art works. And it is his reverence for original structures, whether of objects or of life,

---

1. Isamu Noguchi. *A Sculptor's World* (New York: Harper & Row, 1968).

and their inceptive powers, that makes him say, "I consider most of my works as experimental proposals of concepts."[2]

Isamu Noguchi's actual travels took him through Japan, India, France, America, and other countries. Such travel was very likely predestined. His spirit of near-fastidious self-denial that one reads of in his biographical accounts may have come from inner conflicts arising from the circumstances of his birth. At the same time the urge to search conflicted with his desire to find a place to settle. Thus, he began to travel.

But once begun, his traveling took on a significance beyond the searching of a specific individual. Nor was it the mere inner wandering of a genius. For us it may be called a symbol.

As Fuller pointed out, "The airplane era laid a new cosmic egg in the nest of everyday reality, integrating all the previously separate civilizations' experiences in one history and one geography."[3] Naturally, relationships of lending and borrowing had already developed in various cultures in the past. But at present, when modern Western dominance is facing collapse, they have a different significance.

A mirror is being broken and in each shattered piece different faces are reflected. No longer can you view your image in a single mirror. And a shattered mirror cannot be reassembled.

The idea of integration and of the wholeness of human aspiration is not directed at creating an innocuous, neutral state but at finding oneself among those countless conflicting and irregular shapes. Modern Japan has spent a long time trying to discover itself in the huge Western European mirror, but now that some time has passed, it should try to see itself in those countless fragments of mirror. But the ability to unite those numerous scattered, distorted images is called imagination. And the power to do that requires an act of will.

Those wide expanses—geographic and imaginative—they are there, indistinguishably merged in the travels of Noguchi.

---

2. Noguchi. *A Sculptor's World*, p. 28.
3. R. Buckminster Fuller. Foreword to *A Sculptor's World*, p. 7.

Originally from the catalogue for "Isamu Noguchi—A Retrospective" at Gallery Minami, Tokyo, 1973. From: *Ki no Kagami, Sogen no Kagami* [*Mirror of Tree, Mirror of Field*]. Tokyo: Shinchōsha, 1975.

Redon Fantasy

A Lone Tree in the Wasteland

It is interesting that stages in the evolution of life are symbolically shown in the shape of a tree—a family tree, for example. When I think of Odilon Redon, for some reason I always think of a tree, a lone tree, nameless, standing in the field of life somewhere on the border between light and darkness, yet clearly defined in my consciousness. Perhaps it comes to mind because the tree is so often portrayed in Redon's *noir* series. But this may not be the only reason, since my feelings and thoughts about many of his works so resemble what I feel about trees, their incomparable gentleness and severity—like light and darkness, sky and earth, life and death. As living phenomena trees connect such extremes, something I recognize as a continuous process in Redon's paintings.

Intellectually I agree with J.-M. G. Le Clézio's remark that a tree stands in "continual reproach to the human creature."[1] Today any healthy relationship to trees is rapidly disappearing. At least we seem unable to accommodate trees, seeking only to exploit them for our own advantage. In the days of Redon and Rilke there was still a friendly relationship between people and trees. A tree could grow within a person, painters and poets could stand within a tree and absorb the nourishment of the earth. And the painter's solitude could be reflected in a lone tree in the wasteland. In this solitude there is salvation. But I do not view Redon with simple nostalgia.

I know little about Redon. Generally his *noir* works, referring to his charcoal drawings and lithographs, have been described as dark, gloomy inner visions. But to me they appear as if they are warm, light earth after having absorbed the sunlight, or as a piece of white cloth that, having been spread in the dark night, has evoked and nourished dreams—a world where, after having destroyed all intellectual interpretations, the unconscious now lives and breathes.

Certainly in Redon's *noir* works one can sense unfathomable depths. It is not simply a matter of the black color. It is as if all colors were there together in an extraordinary potentiality. After World War II, by electronic

1. Jean-Marie Gustave Le Clézio. *Conversation avec J.-M. G. Le Clézio,* ed. by Pierre Lhost. Paris: Editions Mercure de France, 1971.

means, we produced and processed sounds that contained all the frequencies. That development changed our traditional attitude, which regarded music as combined sounds and gave rise to expanded ideas of music. We now call that sound "white noise," which comes to mind when I think of Redon's *noir* works. We hear white noise as one sound: however, by further processing we create new sounds. But the importance of comparing white noise to traditional musical sounds is the realization that through white noise we reach sounds inaudible to the human ear—part of what I intuitively call the "river of sound." This idea should remind us of the totality and sensuousness of sound, sound that had become only functional. Perhaps Redon's *noir* is not only black in terms of color but was the best vehicle for him to express his perceptions.

Black and white, usually considered the extremes of color, more correct-ly are extremes of light. While they support our vision they are in a realm beyond our seeing. To reach that realm we must walk the unknown path of the unconscious. Naturally Redon's character as a visionary helped, but his recognition of black as the "true color" came to him quite consciously. He wrote of his theory of visions that arise when serving the invisible. Referring to his gifts from nature that led him to dreams, Redon wrote:

> I submitted to the torments of imagination and the surprises she gave me under my pencil; but I directed and led those surprises in accordance with the laws of the organism of art which I know, which I feel, with the single goal of producing in the spectator, by sudden attraction, the whole evocation, and the whole enticement of the uncertain within the confines of thought.[2]

Reading these words we can understand that Redon was not merely a painter exploring his dark, gloomy inner self. Redon's "black" reaches deep into the distant realm of that "peculiar eye-like balloon moving toward infinity." Then disguising worldly colors appear. Together, these colors and black symbolize the fullness of life and eternal death.

I discovered Redon when shown an art book as I was leaving the atelier

---

2. Odilon Redon, *To Myself: Notes on Life, Art and Artists*, translated from the French by Mira Jacob and Jeanne L. Wasserman (New York: George Braziller, Inc., 1986), p. 21.

of the late graphic artist Tetsurō Komai. At that time Komai was a young rising artist who had begun showing his works in the Shunyōkai exhibition.

It was about thirty years ago. I was still undecided about becoming a composer. As I think back, that art book could have been *Odilon Redon, oeuvres graphiques complètes* [The Hague: G. J. Nieuwenhaizen Segaar, 1913], with rather low-quality reproductions. Spellbound, only nodding to Komai's comment, "Great, isn't it?" I could not take my eyes off that peculiar black-and-white image. Then I noticed the name "Redon" and the title of the work, "Les Origines" ["The Origins"]. It was in that decisive moment that I became interested in visual art.

Since then I have often visited Komai's studio. In observing his work I have witnessed those moments when chance awakens deep desire within the artist with a near-violent force—that mysterious process peculiar to graphic arts—to me a source of mysterious surprise and joy. Twisted, antennae-like lines scratched into polished copper plate reflect a transcendental landscape somewhere beyond time. At such moments I felt a shiver run through me.

As I watched the artist at work, my interest in art deepened and the art of Odilon Redon became a more distinct influence on my sensory antennae.

Looking back, I find I wrote these notes on Redon:

> There, some life beyond time existed quietly, in harmony, telling us of eternity—those violent and cruel powers that form the world are gently captured. That work of Redon's that my friend showed me in his small studio looked like unformed heaven and earth, with a violent primordial energy and anxiety of things being born: an eyeball floating in the dark night, looking like...what? A flower? A human form? In "The Origins" one can see Redon's true qualities purely concentrated in black and white: the movement of the desire in all earthly things as they aspire to evolve into something human, or, the mysterious exchange of feelings that Rilke felt in the swaying trees when he wrote, "I am becoming a tree, or, is the tree becoming me?" Emerging from some deep swamp, that eyeball will haunt me forever. Is that the stare that threatened Cain?

While looking at some of the figure painting in that album Komai showed me, I experienced the same familiarity I feel in Buddhist ink painting or ukiyo-e, traditions that influence many other contemporary painters.

Recently I have had the strange feeling of taking another artist who has affected me intensely, namely Kagaku Murakami, and quite naturally associating him with Redon. Kagaku himself stated that he was influenced by William Blake. Although there is no direct artistic relation between Redon and Blake such as there was between Redon and Klee, both Blake and Redon were European visionaries. I started to wonder if (or perhaps just playfully imagine that) Kagaku had come to know Redon's work at some point. There is no stylistic resemblance, but I feel a psychological connection between these two artists.

Kagaku was a misfit among the *nihonga* [traditional Japanese painting] artists who emphasized nature painting. His isolation and introversion were intensified by his illness. After leaving Kyoto he lived on a local mountainside, painting mountains, trees, the change of seasons. But he felt the importance of expressing an inner world. No other *nihonga* artist achieved the high degree of symbolism shown in Kagaku's late work entitled "Plums and Willows of Early Spring." That work "forever radiates certain mysterious allusions." As a visionary and because of his sickness Kagaku was never able to let his perception play as freely as Redon's. As he penetrated into the spiritual world his perception became almost painful. He once wrote, "My struggling to paint is in fact an effort, however small, to expiate my sins." Kagaku's works came to reflect his almost stifling sense of religious morality.

Kagaku and Redon

Although the artistic accomplishment of Redon and Kagaku cannot be compared, it is interesting to find similarities in these two visionary artists—one from the West, the other from the East. Both attached great significance to sketching. As artists they understood that sketches emphasize pure beauty and are not merely stages or attempts to produce painting. Sketches show us that a world exists beyond the ordinary world we see.

Both Redon and Kagaku were critical of Impressionist painting. Reading his statements in "From My Memoranda," which Kagaku wrote in the eighth year of the Taishō period [1911–1926], I began to think he was even closer to Redon than I had imagined:

> I wish to draw things beyond this world. In short, I wish to create idealistic drawings. It is still a vague desire to which I must give precise color and shape. It may come from a literary source, it may not. As a subject it may be borrowed from the literary, but that is only a proposition and the creation should not be merely descriptive. In painting, the Impressionists eliminated the time element, the human spirit, mystical expressions or dramatic themes of love....

One may compare this passage to something Redon wrote in 1968 criticizing realism, or to his observations on an Impressionist exhibition. But I want to quote what he wrote in his journal about lithographs as an artistic medium following "faith breathing senses":

> Black should be respected. Nothing prostitutes it. It does not please the eye and does not awaken sensuality. It is the agent of the spirit much more than the splendid color of the palette or of the prism. Therefore, a good print will be enjoyed more in a somber country where harsh nature constrains man to be confined at home, cultivating his thought, as in the regions of the North, for example, and not as in those of the South, where the sun draws us outdoors and enchants us.[3]

I read all available writings by Kagaku but could not find one reference to Redon. Still, I am unable to give up my idea that he knew of Redon's work.

Recently, however, I discovered an interesting essay by Norio Awazu entitled "Double Darkness—Redon and Japan." Now I think my association of these two artists may have some foundation. In that essay Awazu documents some surprising information.

Just about that time—around 1920, shortly after Redon's death—artists of the Kyoto Realist School (such as Bakusen Tsuchida, Keigetsu Kikuchi, and Chikkyō Ono, who were traveling in Europe) were all greatly impressed by Redon and bought his works. Bakusen visited the residence of Redon's son, Ari, and is said to have purchased the oil paintings "Young

---

3. Odilon Redon, *To Myself*, pp. 103–104.

Buddha" and "Bouquet of White Flower Petals" and a few sketches. Through the auspices of a gallery, Keigetsu bought the "Portrait of Mme. Redon in Pastels" and a pencil sketch, "Woman's Face." Chikkyō Ono also bought a sketch, and Seihō Takeuchi, the central figure in the Kyoto Realist School, also purchased and brought back to Japan such works as "Girl's Profile among Flowers," "Bouquet with Red Leaves," and a landscape.

According to his biography, after graduating from the Kyoto Shiritsu Kaiga Senmongakkō [Municipal Art School] in Meiji 44 [1912], Kagaku began studying with Seihō Takeuchi. In addition, his technique was strongly influenced by Bakusen Tsuchida. Later he joined the Kokuga Sōsaku Kyōkai [National Creative Association], which included Bakusen and Chikkyō Ono, who were part of that group that had been in Europe. In fact, from Taishō 10 to 12 [1920–22], the leading artists of this group had been to Europe. This is undoubtedly the group Awazu had reported as buyers of Redon's works. With the absence of Bakusen and others, an exhibition of this group's work was postponed until Taishō 14 [1924]. Rimmei Kawakita, in his book *Murakami Kagaku*, reported that the works Kagaku submitted to the fourth Kokuten [exhibition] were small and markedly different from his previous works. This difference made a strong impression on his colleagues, and it was noted that Kagaku remarked, "It is now time for me to change, as I stand at a point of experiencing a spiritual rebirth and must start at once to train my mind."

What could have caused those changes in Kagaku's life? Of course, there may have been reasons within the artist as well as external circumstances. But my assumption is that among those influences, perhaps the strongest may have been those works by Redon that Bakusen Tsuchida brought back from Europe.

Kagaku died in Shōwa Era 14 [1939], on one November day at his home in Hanakuma in Kobe, the image of Redon reflected in his tired eyes.

FROM: *Ongaku no Yohaku kara* [*From the Margin of the Music*]. Tokyo: Shinchōsha, 1980.

Plate 1. Takemitsu at home, 1991. Photo by Tetsuya Fukui.

Arc for Strings is played as a part of *Your Love and the Crossing*, from *Arc for Piano and Orchestra* (Part I).

Performance requires a graphic score, written as a circle (or part of a circle) with thin and thick lines and a dot [Plate 2], and two other instruction cards [Plates 3a and 3b].

> 1. Performance is started from the *dot*, which indicates a pitch. If the dot is placed high on the square paper, the player can choose a high-pitched tone of the instrument as he wishes, and so on.
>
> 2. After the player has decided on a pitch, if he finds that the dot is placed on the thick line, he continues the performance coordinating with the instruction card written (a), (p), (cL), and (cB) [Plate 3a]. It is important to comply with the instructions for the player's quadrant. If a dot falls in the (p) quadrant, for example, it should be played pizzicato.
>
> 3. If the dot is on the thin line, the player should coordinate with the other instruction card in the same manner.
>
> 4. One round takes one minute.
>
> 5. After a round, the graphic score is turned, giving the player a new starting pitch and a new way of performing.
>
> ...to hear *change* as a sound-aspect.
>
> ...to hear the inner movement of sounds.

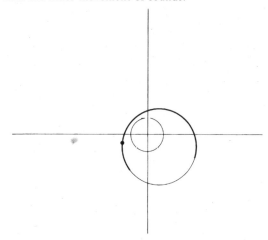

Plate 2. *Arc for Strings*, Copyright © 1963 by Editions Salabert, Paris.

a ─── arco double stops, harmonics
ordinary, sul tasto
sul ponticello, col legno

p ─── pizzicato ordinary bartok pizz.

c Ⓛ ─── col legno

c Ⓑ ─── col legno battuto

●●●● ─── knock the body with finger
knock on the tail-piece with bow

⚏ ─── arco, behind the bridge

⚏ ─── arpeggio, behind the bridge
by pizzicato or col legno

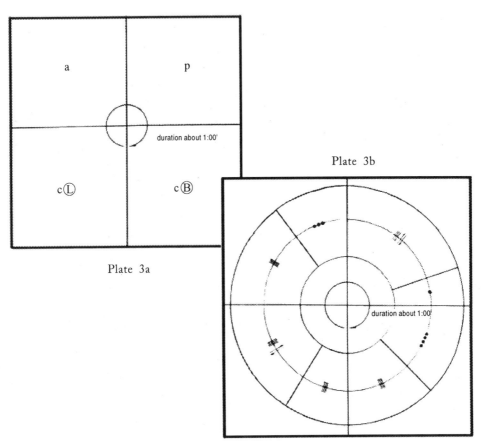

Plate 3b

Plate 3a

Plate 4. Composers of the Experimental Workshop posing for the August 1955 issue of *Geijutsu Shinchō*. With Toru Takemitsu sitting in the foreground; standing, left to right: Hiroyoshi Suzuki, Keijirō Satō, and Jōji Yuasa. From *Experimental Workshop, The 11th Exhibition [in] Homage to Shūzō Takiguchi.* Tokyo: Satani Gallery, 1991, p. 120.

On His Composing

A Personal Approach

One day in 1948 while riding a crowded subway I came up with the idea of mixing random noise with composed music. More precisely, it was then that I became aware that composing is giving meaning to that stream of sounds that penetrates the world we live in.

> **The sour body odor of tired people, myself included. Doors open, disgorging people into the bright outside. Scattering, each his own way, all looking tired. In the subway remote from the outside world, or outside under bright sunlight...there seemed to be no difference. Is this the real way of the modern world?**

The music I composed at that time certainly had nothing to do with people. We were all in our own little worlds, isolated from one another. But I found it increasingly intolerable to work as a composer in such isolation. I craved some kind of relationship to those around me.

If I look at Honegger's pessimistic point of view from the other way around, wasn't he saying that it is not people who are indifferent and lack understanding toward music, rather it is music that lacks meaning in people's lives?

Contemporary music stands apart from the lives of ordinary people. But why has present-day music become so isolated?

Basically music depends on mathematical organization. Through no fault of his own, the composer exercises his mathematical alchemy in pursuit of universal beauty. But our task, not limited only to music, is to reveal things that come to us through our spiritual efforts. Art is nothing but the actualization of the creative spirit. Pieces of music are facts captured by the spirit, using sound as a medium. In that sense pieces of music are concrete things. We often hear that music is abstract, but this is a vague and misleading statement. I would not deny the abstract nature of sounds, but compositions should be concrete in terms of conveying vivid musical impressions.

As I mentioned, music is based on mathematical organization and, unlike other types of creation, involves unique time elements. Because of this the form as art work becomes important. It is important that compositional methods always be directed toward the search for the inner spirituality of man. It would be an extreme error if the composer limited himself to the search for external formulas.

The music I am discussing here is European music, which is realized within a highly organized system. A long time has passed since music was established as an art in Europe. During that time composers gradually replaced the real essence of music with a derivative search for technique. This tendency toward specialized classification is evident not only in music but in European rationalism generally, and it was in this mathematical alchemy that composers lost the real essence of music.

The twelve-tone method of composition may be the result of historical necessity, but it presents some very dangerous aspects. The mathematical and geometric pursuit of sound apparent in this technique is purely an intellectual act. It can result in the same weaknesses as those that arise in any overspecialized aesthetic purity. It carries with it the danger of hardening perceptions, and it is the perceptions that are the basic elements in creativity. Of course we should have the courage to discover new systems and face new methods. But we should not forget that these things must be dealt with by human hands.

In the dim lights of the subway I was conscious only of the rhythm of the train and its physical effect on me. I was thinking about music, or I should say more precisely I was thinking about sounds themselves quite apart from any obscure meaning or function in music.

Within an organized system sounds are bound and forced by mathematics and physics. Composers have been too steeped in techniques, trying to grasp sounds only through their function within the system. I believe, however, that the task of the composer should begin with the recognition and experience of the more basic sounds themselves rather than with concern about their function.

When I face the sun I sneeze. Is this really a silly comment, having nothing to do with music? And was it wrong of me to have felt a particular agony in the sound of the door someone closed?

The regular rhythm of the train coursed through our bodies, pounded inside our perspiring skins; and I and the others in the subway leaned on this rhythm, receiving some kind of rest from it.

Music was born in primal utterance and action. But in our long history we have come to understand sounds only within the limitations of conventional function. That rich world of sound around me ... those are the sounds that I should have the courage to let live within my music. To reconcile those diverse, sometimes contradictory, sounds around us, that is the exercise we need in order to walk that magical and miraculous road we call life.

Sound is continuous, unbroken movement. If we understand it that way, conventional notation, which divides sound into discrete measures, is fruitless.

> The train stopped at a station. Passengers entered and left. Then again in the fast-moving train people settled down, regaining that repose from the regular vibrations.
>
> We passed through a dark tunnel. I thought of returning to the womb, back to one's origin. What is the difference between being a cave dweller and a passenger on a modern subway? The subway has concrete, rails, and rivets. That is the difference. Not much difference from a cave dwelling. But the images I had of that subway tunnel and a cave were quite different. Those parallel rails carried many people, all slightly tired.

In ancient times man had to fight for survival. Those who fought were real men. They beat back those who threatened them as well as the hostile universe. War and song. Simple acts of life and song. Fear and prayer. Joy and prayer.

The correspondence between the inner and outer lives of those ancient people was splendid. They related to trees, stones, sky. And poetry, religion, song, and dance existed as an undivided unity, all united with the act of fighting. Perhaps those things preceded art, but their elegant power grips my imagination.

But modern man no longer chants his magical incantations. Have the magical powers deserted us? Not action, but expression now? Must I endure the falseness in art?

> Standing in those dim subway lights I was as weary as the other passengers. I found myself wishing for a more direct relationship to the people around me.

It came to me as a revelation: bring noise into the realm of organized music.

I recorded various sounds and frequencies on tape. Surrounded by these random sounds I found they triggered emotional responses in me, which, in turn, I preserved as sound on tape. I conceived of my approach as something akin to action rather than to expression.

In 1948 the French composer Pierre Schaeffer first composed *musique concrète*, based on the same ideas as mine. This was a happy coincidence for me. Music was changing, slightly perhaps, but nevertheless changing.

I left the subway and walked into the bright outside. That statue of the silent dog in the park seemed so meaningless.

FROM: *OTO CHINMOKU TO HAKARIAERUHODONI* [*SOUND: CONFRONTING THE SILENCE*]. TOKYO: SHINCHŌSHA, 1971.

Notes on November Steps

From March until early fall, 1967, I had a studio in a small resort in Nagano Prefecture. I was staying there while working on a piece commissioned by the New York Philharmonic for their 125th anniversary.

It was spring, and the wind was still cold. I had with me two scores by Debussy, *Prélude à "L'Après-midi d'un faune"* and *Jeux*. The score for the prelude was a piano reduction in the composer's own handwriting. The notes were in soft green, rose, and brown ink, on a fine-quality yellowish paper. A number of changes had been made, with marginal notes in fine pink lines. Although a score is, in the usual sense, a hypothetical plan, as I looked at the composer's marks on that score they took on a vivid life of their own. I wonder... were those handwritten symbols that appeared as half-erased stains on the paper really only hypothetical?

In September I completed a piece called *November Steps*. In October I caught a flight from Haneda airport in order to be in New York for the premiere performance.

— *1. Making Sound* —

Among those people who have no written language there is a much closer relationship between sounds and the meaning or content of those sounds. There is a beautiful harmony in such a relationship. Without written symbols, the vocabulary is limited but the words have greater flexibility in meaning. They take on variety through the simple process of making different sounds and linking them together.

In the language of the Hawaiians and Polynesians, for example, meanings are changed by the different ways of breathing while speaking. Because of this the words have a wide range of delicate inflections. Also in the Ainu language one word can have many meanings. Such multiplicity gives a rich expressiveness to speech. In the same way, the simple repetitions in Swahili sound musical. Silence is the womb from which such languages are born. Their lives are sustained by being spoken. A single word may have manifold, contradictory meanings.

Words are the reservoir of imagination from which we continue to draw fresh water. In this case, uttering sound is a communicative act based on two aspects: the intellectual-sensual quality of the words themselves, and the ordinary or extraordinary experiences we attach to those words. In this way words are filled with meaning beyond their actual capacity.

Our vocabulary abounds in words, but they usually serve abstract purposes. If words are never uttered as sound they can never transcend their limited capacity as designators.

— 2. IMAGINATION: LISTENING TO AND RECOGNIZING SOUND —

In music not all sounds are restricted to being functional. As all living things have their own innate cycles, visible and invisible, so it is with sounds. Each sound has its own beautiful form and order, like a living cell. Sounds undergo constant change in the perspective of time. Their division into regular and irregular sounds has nothing to do with their real nature. There is a point of view holding that irregular sound (commonly called noise) is an unpleasant signal that disturbs our hearing. Sometimes dissonant sounds are referred to as irregular. But the problem here is that the dissonance of one stylistic period can be experienced as consonance in another period. In the history of Western music the earliest dissonant sound was the tritone, the same interval that has become our most recent consonance. In contrast to noise, musical sound is usually construed to be a physiologically conditioned and controlled sound signal. Would other kinds of music with delicate nuances outside this controlled system be experienced by Western ears as noise?

When we are in a natural setting the extraneous sounds we hear and the singing of birds seem to have the same value. In such a natural environment the natural noises do not interfere with our listening. The reverberations of those countless sounds actually assist our listening. Lively and variegated natural sounds coexist in space as something that requires no outside complement.

There are different musical traditions outside Europe that approach these natural conditions. In the flow of Japanese music, for example, short fragmented connections of sounds are complete in themselves. Those different sound events are related by silences that aim at creating a harmony of events. Those pauses are left to the performer's discretion. In this way there is a dynamic change in the sounds as they are constantly reborn in new relationships. Here the role of the performer is not to produce sound but to listen to it, to strive constantly to discover sound in silence. Listening is as real as making sound; the two are inseparable. When John Cage talked to Master Wadatsumi, the famous *hōchiku*[1] player, he wrote these words, which were published in the magazine *Sekai*:

> I decided to use a contact microphone in order to introduce an electrical circuit into the music. The results were quite interesting. If you touch this microphone to wood it picks up the vibrations of the wood itself, bringing them into audible range. Through this scientific achievement new sounds can be heard. For example, by touching the microphone to a wall, a pillar, a table, or to bamboo, sounds never before heard become audible.

Such an idea is related to experimentation in Western music, a tradition that has constantly been experimenting. What makes it so interesting is that this is done not to divide art and life, but to unite them. Such sounds come as a revelation to us.

Since sounds move in time, they are constantly around us, freshly reborn with each appearance. But we may not realize this because of our own laziness. Also, our ears, confined by the conventions of organized music, do not try to hear these sounds in the right way. Musical imagination, so long in the grips of self-expression, hears these sounds only as a means to expand self-expression.

Sounds are ever-present as new individual realities. Let us start listening with unfettered ears. Soon sounds will reveal their turbulent transformations to us.

Imaginative hearing consists of listening to and recognizing sounds in their true nature.

— *3. ADDENDA* —

1. Whatever it is that draws me to music, it is an inner, highly personal force with very little influence from the outside. That is not to say there is never an external influence. But if there is, only a small part of it comes to me as an immediate influence. And then, it is only after I enlarge and transform that small part into an inner force that it becomes a part of my musical imagination.

---

1. A bamboo flute, similar to the *shakuhachi*, but larger in diameter.

2. In writing I frequently use the word "nature." For me it is a kind of calling out to the world. Nature is adjective, adverb, and noun, an imaginative force that actively comes at me. For me, music—whether of the East or the West—in its natural state has this imaginative force.

3. Many contemporary works seem to avoid the "past." This is not one of my concerns. The new and the old are both necessary to me.

But the "unknown" is neither past nor future. It exists only in the precise present.

4. My own modes of musical thoughts follow the natural inclination of sounds. I have no precompositional assumptions. It is not that I try to make sounds themselves the medium. But when I make those sounds speak to me something happens in the act of composition: they change from something that merely exists to something dynamic.

5. For *Notations*, edited by John Cage, I wrote the following:[2]

> I recognize in notation the same sort of phenomenon as there is in the growth of a constellation or a plant.
>
> There, the most important *changes* cannot be perceived directly, visually. In notation, the coexistence of change and possibility. (Also impossibility.)

— *4.* —

Memoranda from the New York Philharmonic Association kept arriving asking for the title of my work. I had already submitted titles on two separate occasions, then changed my mind and withdrew them.

Music exists as a pre-nominative state. A title should be precise but not limiting, strongly evocative, but still leaving some room for imagination.

The nature that surrounds us in the world is nameless. By naming or addressing a thing it becomes part of us. When we call a tree a tree, beauty emerges in its primal form. When cut, sawed, and planed, that beauty becomes clearer. When a house is built of that wood its beauty becomes an everyday thing. I kept the list of titles I had suggested to myself. They

2. The comments in this form appear in English in the original Japanese publication. However, Takemitsu's comments in Cage's book—John Cage, *Notations* (New York: Something Else Press, 1969)—vary somewhat from those cited here.

all were related to things that had influenced me: REFLECTION ... VORTEX ... FLOWER ... SATURATION ... WATER RINGS....

It was this last title, *Water Rings*, that seemed to grow inside my vague musings. In my mountain cabin the sounds that reached me always echoed, varying with weather conditions. Since I intended to use this idea of sound in my music, the title *Water Rings* seemed appropriate at the time.

For me the sound of *biwa* and *shakuhachi* was to spread through the orchestra gradually enlarging, like waves of water. When I mentioned this to my friend Jasper Johns he told me that "water rings" in the United States usually referred to those rings left in a dirty bathtub. So when I explained exactly what I did mean he said he understood, but most Americans would not associate the title with my meaning. Naturally, I followed Johns's advice, and in fact, I was not disappointed that my original title with its metaphysical connotations referred to bathtub rings. Indeed, the language, thoughts, and feelings of the different world cultures do not distress me. On the contrary, we need these things to make our day-to-day life work.

I continued to write titles. After writing them it was as if a second, unknown part of me reacted to them. Steadily, slowly, my thoughts focussed.

I decided on the title *November Steps*.

— 5. —

1. A composer should not be occupied by such things as how one blends traditional Japanese instruments with an orchestra. Two worlds of sound: *biwa–shakuhachi* and the orchestra. Through juxtaposition it is the difference between the two that should be emphasized.

2. To create several different audio foci is one aspect (an objective one) of composing. And to try to hear a specific voice among numerous sounds is yet another.

3. Sound in Western music progresses horizontally. But the sound of the *shakuhachi* rises vertically, like a tree.

4. Do you know that the ultimate achievement the *shakuhachi* master strives for in his performance is the re-creation of the sound of wind blowing through an old bamboo grove?

5. First concentrate on the simple act of listening. Only then can you comprehend the aspirations of the sounds themselves.

6. There is something suggestive in the biologists' report that the dolphins' communication takes place, not in their sounds, but in the length of silences between the sounds.

7. Like time zones on the globe, arrange the orchestra in several time zones—a spectrum of time.

8. A composition should not give the impression it is complete in itself. Which is more pleasurable, a precisely planned tour or a spontaneous trip?

9. Many contemporary composers have been building walls of sounds following their own clever devices. But then, who lives inside those rooms?

10. Eleven steps without any special melodic scheme ... constantly swaying impulses, like those in Noh drama.

11. *November Steps*, commissioned by the New York Philharmonic for its 125th anniversary, premiered in November, 1967 by that orchestra.

— *6. NOVEMBER STEPS* —

The New York Philharmonic is a superb orchestra but it has its conservative side. As in the case of many other orchestras, it is common for an indescribable tension and antagonism to develop between the composer and the performers when a new work is performed. In facing new music that attempts to destroy orchestral conventions many years in the making, the orchestra, as an easy way out, collectively chooses to deny the work rather than trying to understand why the composer had to do what he did. Many performers do not participate creatively in their performing art. This tendency is particularly evident in orchestras.

But the problem is not only with orchestras. If a composer hopes actively to communicate with the listener he must pay more attention to his relationship with the performer. The orchestra, or any performer for that matter, functions as a human organ trying to carry the composer's message. In addition, it may also be an organ that receives communications from the listeners. As a composer, it is by listening to the orchestra, this active and at the same time passive human organ, that I affirm my own ideas.

This particular work had four New York performances. Through these hearings the work gradually changed its character within me, preparing me for yet another step.

I entered the Philharmonic Hall at Lincoln Center with Kinshi Tsuruta, the *biwa* player, and Katsuya Yokoyama, the *shakuhachi* player. They had come with me from Japan for the premiere performance. The first rehearsal began. Since we had had one rehearsal with the Toronto Symphony, of which Seiji Ozawa was musical director, we were not very worried. *Biwa* and *shakuhachi* with their centuries of tradition, the New York Philharmonic with its 125 years of tradition, the still-youthful Seiji Ozawa, and myself—a curiously interesting combination.

At first I had considerable reservations about using *biwa* and *shakuhachi* in this new work. Perhaps the fact that it was to be premiered in the United States concerned me in that I feared it might be taken as just another exotic work. Then too, I thought it might be foolish to waste my own efforts in experiments in mixing traditional Japanese with Western music. Last year I wrote *Eclipse* for *biwa* and *shakuhachi*. That was not as much an experiment with these instruments as it was an attempt to tap the demonic powers locked up in them. Impressed by the performance of Tsuruta and Yokoyama, I found my world of sound widened and deepened.

I received the commission from the New York Philharmonic and knew that Seiji Ozawa would be the conductor. I conferred with him about the work and we were able to speak quite frankly about the problems. After hearing *Eclipse* and being fully aware of the dangers of using traditional Japanese instruments with orchestra, it was he who suggested that I write for *biwa* and *shakuhachi*. At one point he remarked to me, "You are not writing a special kind of Japanese music. No one else will be responsible if it ends up sounding exotic."

The score for this work has numerous passages where there are extremely fine divisions sounding together but with very troublesome instructions about relative changes in volume of sound. Just as Seiji Ozawa had remarked that "the New York Philharmonic is hostile toward contemporary music," some performers openly demonstrated their antagonism as the opening of the piece was rehearsed. Ozawa stopped the disturbed orchestra to explain the nature of the sound I had in mind, using very precise instructions. I was optimistic about the specific techniques I had employed but a little disappointed in the general results. In contrast to the belligerent mood of the orchestra, Tsuruta and Yokoyama sat serenely with closed eyes. After the opening section the *biwa* and *shakuhachi* entered. The mood of the orchestra began changing, slowly, but nevertheless changing. The orchestra sound came alive, as if something beyond technique had been added.

November Steps has a section near the end where only the Japanese instruments play. During the eight minutes or so that it lasted the orchestra members listened intently. Yes, of course there was a curiosity about the "mysterious East." But there was something more than that. They were enchanted by the music of two fine performers. The final orchestral coda was so alive that it was hard to imagine that it was played by the same orchestra that had begun the piece.

After the designated final silence, bravos and applause exploded from the orchestra.

I walked along the West Side in the chilly New York evening. I wanted to be alone to relive that excitement that had welled up inside of me.

My first New York November steps had finally been taken.

FROM: *OTO CHINMOKU TO HAKARIAERUHODONI* [*SOUND: CONFRONTING THE SILENCE*]. TOKYO: SHINCHŌSHA, 1971.

Mirror and Egg

This is an edited and expanded version of notes originally written in English for a lecture to a small group of composition students at Yale University in March, 1975. It avoids special musical terms as much as possible. At the same time it may have lost some of the immediacy of the original spoken version. It was presented in rather special circumstances in that it reflected my personal point of view at that time.—*Author's note.*

— *1. Mirror and Egg* —

We can analyze a finished piece of music, but there will be something of that music that escapes our analysis. If music is something that moves us, the mystery is even deeper. Of course I do not believe analysis is meaningless.

I am aware of the great benefits we have gained from contemporary analysis of the human body, for example. Now, through minute DNA, we know of that immense and universal system we all share—yet, we do not understand the power that creates life. And in that ignorance we turn to music—an act that will continue in life and in intelligence yet to come.

Just as people lack self-awareness, there are also many unknowns in music. This also applies to nations that show various unconscious differences.

As a composer I have studied modern Western music. Through works by many composers and fine performances of their music I have come to know their accomplishments—a different tradition from that into which I was born.

I do not compose for simple personal gain but to be reassured of my own being and to explore my relationship to others. Naturally, as one growing up in Japan I could not be independent of my country's traditions. But that awareness of my own national tradition has special meaning, since it came to me after I had studied modern Western music.

There is no doubt, as Buckminster Fuller pointed out, that from the early twentieth century (especially after 1930, with the rapid development of the airplane), the various countries and cultures of the world have begun a journey toward the geographic and historic unity of all peoples.[1] And

---

1. Buckminster Fuller. Foreword for Isamu Noguchi's *A Sculptor's World* (New York: Harper & Row; London: Thames & Hudson, 1968), p. 7.

now all of us, individually and collectively, share in incubating that vast universal cultural egg.

For me, a Japanese, the West was a single enormous mirror. The strong reflected light of that mirror overwhelmed the light of other cultures. But since I became aware of Japanese traditions, quite naturally I became interested in the reflections of other mirrors. Japanese culture reflects the influence of those other mirrors.

Of course cultures have been borrowing and lending for a long time, but those that are completely different from European culture still exist without any signs of decline. The music of China, Korea, India, Thailand, Indonesia, and many other countries continues to attract us endlessly. And it is meaningless to compare their value to that of modern European music, or to make that simple division into East and West. Indian and Japanese music, for example, are generally referred to as "Eastern," but they are quite different. Naturally they have influenced each other and at the same time have developed their own distinctive characters.

About a century ago, Japan began to absorb Western culture. Aggressively it sought the modern technology that Europe had been developing since the Industrial Revolution. Since this was done at such a great speed, certain warping occurred as the government tried to introduce both technological and cultural changes. It was some time after World War II that the conservatories began to teach traditional Japanese music, with the result that you might find the bizarre situation in which a student studying *koto* could not graduate because of insufficient piano technique.

It is true, of course, that many of the Japanese intelligentsia had a deep craving for Western culture, intensified by many years under a feudal system during which they longed for a breath of fresh air. That was the force of history. But history is not merely chronological movement. It is the active course of human energy, something like blood in an artery. I do not deny my country's adoption of Western culture in the last century (to do that would be to deny my own presence), but I have many criticisms of the way in which it was done.

Japan and I have arrived at the present with great contradictions. Political attempts to resolve those contradictions may bring on a crisis and, indeed, may not be possible.

Speaking from my own intuition, rather than from a simple-minded resolution to blend Western and Japanese elements, I choose to confront those contradictions, even intensify them. And those contradictions are for me a valid visa for the world. That is my act of expression.

It is extremely easy for Western music to adapt traditional Japanese music. It is not difficult to blend the two. I have no interest in either of these procedures.

It may sound old fashioned, but I think music still has the power to affect people's lives. It is also extremely personal.

Nothing that truly moves us will come from the superficial blending of East and West. Such music will just sit there.

I need not lecture on the processes of modern Western music of the recent past nor comment on the current confusion. I, too, am in the middle of that confused scene and may even have contributed to it in some small way. I neither approve nor disapprove of the obvious Eastern influences on modern Western music since 1950. I feel the same way toward a certain Romanticism I find in the faithful believers in electronics and toward music that may appear to be new and different but is self-contradictory. To me those composers are somehow cowardly as they face their own traditions.

Certainly now the dictating position of modern Europe has declined, and that huge mirror that reflected my own image has been shattered. And at the same time many Western composers have come to notice the reflections of other mirrors previously overlooked—a necessary development perhaps, but to me it appears to be too hasty.

In political logic, denial is negative and absolute; but to apply political logic to art is to misunderstand its real nature. Without resorting to simple-minded compromise or adjustment, allowing the coexistence of contradiction—theoretically illogical perhaps, but very important—is at the core of meaning in art. And this should not be done solely by feeling, because art is also partly objective and needs a firm logical basis.

To hatch this universal egg we all incubate, perhaps the current trial-and-error approach is necessary. Anyhow, the centuries of modern European music, which is such a brief time in the history of music, is still a tradition too long to be ignored completely.

A year ago I traveled to Indonesia with a group of French musicians. During that visit, after hearing a Javanese gamelan, one of them started talking to me, very excited about the "absolute new resource" in music. His excitement struck me as very strange because I knew that many decades earlier it was the French composer Debussy who, after hearing a gamelan performance in Paris, was profoundly influenced by that music. Moreover, the logical sense of Debussy's music was strengthened by that experience.

In hearing unknown new music, surprise and excitement are most important. Music is not a static art: it is constantly born anew. If this is true, while an electronic recording of the drone in Indian music is not necessarily bad in that it may broaden our musical experience, it really does nothing beyond that.

In the same spirit as the comment by that French musician, to us Western music is still a new resource. In other words, modern European music, along with other kinds of music, is one part of the musical resources today—probably nothing more, nothing less.

Speaking for myself, in contrast to John Cage this recognition came to me in learning Western music. For that reason I am even more concerned than John Cage is about the future of Western music.

This may sound contradictory, but if it is, it is still a profound truth to me. Unless based on a deeper experience of the old, confronting the new will not result in a universal world of new sound. Without a conscious effort music will be static.

To replace the great shattered mirror of Western music, to include the reflections of other mirrors—that is our task today. This may be a creative task possible only in music.

Only in the nest of accumulated individual imaginations will our universal egg hatch.

My words may have been a bit too abstract. Anyway, our imaginative power does not arise from "bespectacled murmuring" but begins with our contact with sounds.

— 2. The Garden of Music —

Arc for Piano and Orchestra was composed in 1963. As I wrote this work many compositional ideas came to me from old Japanese gardens.

I love gardens. They do not reject people. There one can walk freely, pause to view the entire garden, or gaze at a single tree. Plants, rocks, and sand show changes, constant changes.

For *Arc* I divided the orchestra into four solo instrumental groups, namely woodwinds, strings, brass, and percussion. Different roles were assigned to each group. The solo piano assumes the role of an observer strolling through the garden. In the same way that plants and sand exist in a given space in their own time, changing with the climate and season, and that the entire garden is affected by the change from day to night, so do musical aspects change in this piece.

The structure of the piece is shown in Figure 1. Time elements, of course, cannot be shown here since they change with the relative position of the "strolling" piano.

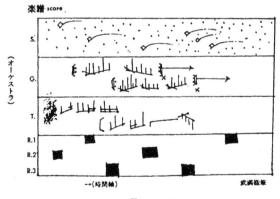

Figure 1

I. Grass and flowers: a group of undetermined soloistic, rapidly changing mobile forms. These solo parts recur in heterocyclic time relation.

II. Trees: do not change as rapidly as grass and flowers. This group, however, is composed as an indeterminate, gradually changing mobile.

III. Rocks: unchanging except as they appear from different viewpoints. These are written as stable forms in a determinate manner as a type of timbral variations.

IV. Sand and earth: enduring and stable, exist unaffected by the total tempo. This is a metagalaxy, a role taken by the percussion.

These are the four groups used in composing *Arc*.

Areas of tempo vary. There are the two tempi for solo instruments, the personal tempo for the solo piano, and the conductor's tempo. There is an orderly overlap of these tempi with a certain discretion allowed the performers, resembling a continual change of pulse.

Arc is a musical garden that changes with each performance. In this metaphysical garden I tried to create a structure of tempo strongly influenced by the traditional idea of *ma*, which exists at the performer's discretion in the Noh drama. Also, by allowing the solo piano to stroll through the garden with changing viewpoints, the piece is freed from a set frame. It becomes a mobile strongly reminiscent of the Heian period [794–1185] handscroll painting.

Such a concept, which gives mode and rhythm to individual parts like characters in a play, comes out of the tradition and musical spirit of Debussy and Messiaen.

The old and new exist within me with equal weight. There is, however, no passive surrender. In the process of creation the stable balance of the two gives way to an active, strong exchange between them; otherwise they would be insignificant. The Mother of Creation does not dwell outside but lives within.

This I call reality.

FROM: *Ongaku no Yohaku kara* [*From the Margin of the Music*]. Tokyo: Shinchōsha, 1980.

Dream and Number

— *I.* —

FROM A LECTURE GIVEN AT STUDIO 200 IN TOKYO ON APRIL 30, 1984

In the past I have not tried to explain my own work in detail. Explanation is not necessary, since the music is there and speaks for itself. Program notes place emphasis on reading and may interfere with the actual hearing of music. Too much explanation may even change the direction of the music and occasionally even inhibit the evocative powers of music. It is the business of music critics to write words, and they may be interested in a composer's words; but I wish music to be experienced with ears.

It is, however, incorrect to say I do not think of music in terms of words. For me composition always involves a strong interaction between music and words. To find an appropriate title for a composition I move back and forth between sounds and words. Many of my titles are strange; some critics think they are simply the result of a poetic whim. But when I decide on a title, it is not merely to suggest a mood but a mark of the significance of the music and the problems encountered in its general construction. Words are the means by which I replace emotion and conflict with a musical plan.

The title of my work, *A Flock Descends into the Pentagonal Garden*, is based on a strange dream; that dream also refers to those vague urges within me that I seek to clarify musically through something as simple as numbers.

The same spring in which I received a commission from the San Francisco Symphony Orchestra, there was a large retrospective show of works by Marcel Duchamp at the Pompidou Center in Paris. I feel my dream was influenced by a portrait of Duchamp by Man Ray included in that exhibit. This photograph shows Duchamp's head with a star shape shaved on its crown.

The night after seeing that photo I dreamt of a pentagonal garden. Flying down and into that garden were countless white birds led by a single black bird. I rarely dream; perhaps that is why the impression left was so strong. When I awoke, that landscape felt very musical, and I wanted to turn it into a composition. For a long time afterward I relived the dream, making precise notes of the memories it evoked. The title somehow emerged: *A Flock Descends into the Pentagonal Garden.*

This childlike drawing of birds is my impression of the dream. When I drew this I happened to remember that old jazz tune, "Bye Bye, Blackbird." Near the blackbird in the center is the note F♯. This bird leading the flock began to play a major role in my thinking. The note F♯ was to become a nucleus in the music (Figure 2).

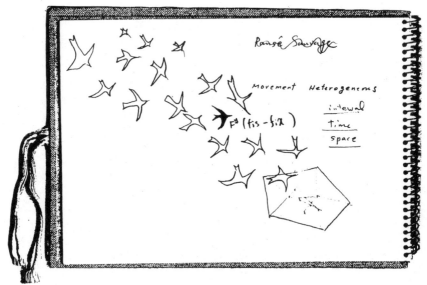

Figure 2

I decided to use an English title, since the work was commissioned by an American orchestra. The general idea was to describe birds flying down into a star-shaped garden, but for the title I sought the advice of my American friend, Roger Reynolds. His first suggestion, "A Flock Settles in a Pentagonal Garden," emphasized neither "birds" nor "garden." Among the possibilities I finally chose "A Flock Descends...," which emphasized the action of the birds. By means of this title I meant to suggest visual space. Figures 3, 4, and 5 show a section of my original piano sketch and two pages from the published score.

Figure 3. *A Flock Descends into the Pentagonal Garden*, © 1977 by Editions Salabert, Paris.

Figure 4. *A Flock Descends into the Pentagonal Garden*, © 1977 by Editions Salabert, Paris.

Figure 5. *A Flock Descends into the Pentagonal Garden*, © 1977 by Editions Salabert, Paris.

The human's eyes and ears are positioned at the same level, not by accident since, if we believe God exists, God created us that way. Eyes and ears. There is a line by Francis Ponge: "The world and all exists in this small space between eyes and ears." But when I hear sound, maybe because I am a visual person, I always have visions. And when I see, I always hear. These are not isolated experiences but always simultaneous, activating imagination. For humans, the relationship between eyes and ears is extremely close.

Perhaps I am mistaken, but a child's eyes, for example, are lower than its ears. In an adult, on the other hand, the eyes are higher. I think there is a tendency for intelligent persons to have eyes higher than ears. Perhaps in the beginning we measured the world through sound, then gradually as the eyes developed and we began to read, the eyes grew closer to the ears and finally surpassed them in importance.

My interest in manipulating numbers is not directed at creating music theory. On the contrary, by using numbers I want to integrate music with the real, changing world. By means of numbers I want to see more clearly those unpredictable, formless images within me that, perhaps prepared over a long time, suddenly emerge in a dream. Through the absolute simplicity of numbers I want to clarify the complexities of the dream. Since I am not a mathematician I react to numbers quite instinctively, and I feel that when they are grasped instinctively, numbers become more cosmological. I say this because I recently visited the reconstructed Katsura Detached Palace in Kyoto. Numerical elements are found there. For example, the *tatami* and *shōji* clearly were planned and constructed according to a numerical plan. Furthermore, the plan is quite instinctively grasped when seen. I was greatly impressed.

Such relationships are also found in Asian music. The Indonesian *ketchak* and the Indian *tala*, for example, are regarded by outsiders as complex numerical constructions, but for native musicians they are practiced instinctively as universal musical ideas. For me, numbers represent color and light.

In *A Flock Descends into the Pentagonal Garden*, the five-sided, star-shaped garden in my dream is an important image. All of the harmonic pitches and fields are based on the number five. I instantly thought of the pentatonic African and Oriental scale, or the black keys of the piano: C♯, E♭, F♯, A♭, and B♭, with F♯ as the central pitch. In German that pitch is *Fis*, which sounds something like the English "fix"; and with the intentional pun in mind, I use that F♯ as a fixed drone. When we look at the intervals between notes in the pentatonic scale, we see the succession of diminished third, augmented second, diminished third, major second, augmented third [shown, according to Japanese convention, as +2, -3, +2, +2, and -3 in Figure 6].

Figure 6

In Figure 7, I show this succession of 2, 3, 2, 2, 3 semitones in a simple magic square.[1]

	0	1	2	3	4	5
C♩		+2	−3	+2	+2	−3
E♭		−3	+2	+2	−3	+2
(fix)F♩		+2	+2	−3	+2	−3
A♭		+2	−3	+2	−3	+2
B♭		−3	+2	−3	+2	+2

Figure 7

1. A literal translation of the author's discussion would create some confusion, since his terminology substitutes enharmonic equivalents, e.g., diminished third and augmented second.

Starting from the central point, F♯ (Fix), these semitone sequences will generate E♭ and C♯ in one direction [Figure 7, upward from F♯ in left column; also Figure 8a]. Conversely, they will generate A♭, B♭ below, and the octave C♯ in the other direction [Figure 7, downward from F♯ in the left column; also Figure 8a]. If we take C♯, for example [descending

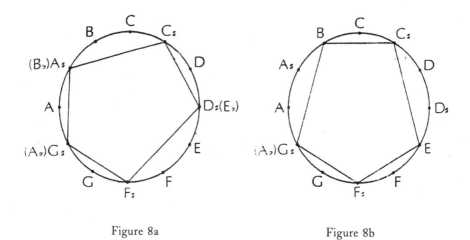

Figure 8a   Figure 8b

expansion, according to Figure 9], the first major second downward is B [according to the horizontal sequence of 2, 3, 2, 2, 3 semitones in Figure 7], followed by A♭ (G♯), F♯, E, and the lower octave, C♯. This is shown in Figures 8b and 9.

Following the chart in Figure 7, the individual pitches [0–5] of each scale [left column] projected by ascending or descending expansion [A♭, B♭ ascend, F♯, E♭, C♯ descend, following the sequence of semitones in its horizontal line] will combine to make the chords seen in Figure 10.

Chords 0 and 5 in Figure 10 contain the same five pitches but have extremely different registers. And in the five different scales found in Figure 7, F♯ sounds as a drone. And to each scale fundamental [column 0 in Figure 7], I add the inverted basic pentatonic scale like grapes clustering down. I show all of that in Figure 11. Five harmonic fields are analogous to the pentagonal garden.

Figure 9

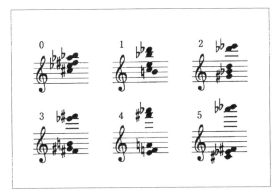

Figure 10

The pages from the last part of the piece (Figures 12, 13, and 14) depict the pentagonal garden and the flock of birds descending through the clouds. All the musical elements of the piece are presented in these sounds. At the opening, the oboes present the theme of the flock (Figure 15). This is also based on the same pitches.

After this theme the birds begin flying—a dreamy, uncertain, sometimes dangerous flight—before descending into the garden. The theme of the flock appears and the work ends.

. . . . .

Figure 11

In my music there is no constant development as in the sonata; instead, imaginary soundscapes appear. A single element is never emphasized with development through contrast. The listener need not understand the different operations discussed here. Actually I have my own theories of structure and systematic procedure, but I wish to avoid overemphasizing these. My music is composed as if fragments were thrown together unstructured, as in dreams. You go to a far place and suddenly find yourself back home without having noticed the return.

When thinking of music, I see symbols on flat paper and grasp them as notes. But in the case of my music, unless these notes are performed and take shape in sound they have no significance. If only correct theory exists, then sounds do not have their own being. For me, sounds are the

Figure 12. *A Flock Descends into the Pentagonal Garden*, © 1977 by Editions Salabert, Paris.

Figure 13. *A Flock Descends into the Pentagonal Garden,* © 1977 by Editions Salabert, Paris.

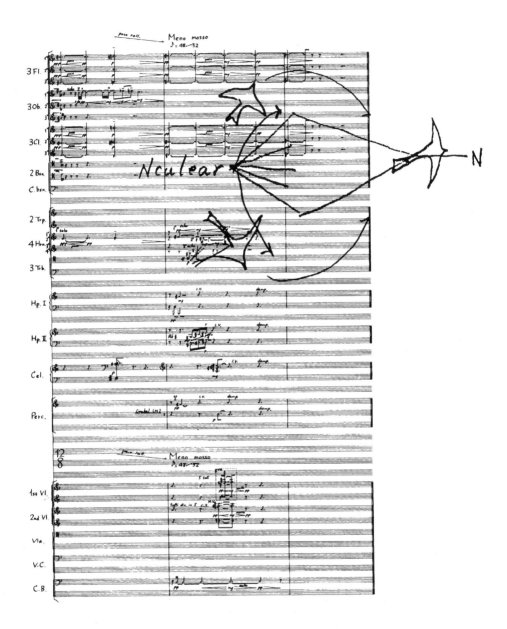

Figure 14. *A Flock Descends into the Pentagonal Garden*, © 1977 by Editions Salabert, Paris.

Figure 15. *A Flock Descends into the Pentagonal Garden*, © 1977 by Editions Salabert, Paris.

essence, and all theoretical systems exist with these sounds in mind.

In the fugal technique of Johann Sebastian Bach, structure is very important. When played by any instrument, that musical structure remains essential and will not be destroyed. In my case it is quite different. I learned much from the music of Debussy. (Of course, I studied in my own way, but I think of him as my great mentor.) While his music can be analyzed in different ways, his greatest contribution was his unique orchestration, which emphasizes color, light, and shadow. Unlike the orchestration of German composers, that of Debussy has many musical focuses. Of course, he was European with sensibilities different from mine, yet he learned from both Japan and the West, and his individuality created a unique sense of orchestration. And that is what I learned from him.

His music is unique in that, rather than emphasizing one principal theme, it displays multiple aspects of sound. This may have something to do with French music, which—compared to German music by such composers as Bach—shows special attention to color. For example, in French organ registration, the sturdy middle range is in perfect balance with the upper and lower registers. Debussy follows the coloristic tradition of composers such as Couperin, Rameau, and Lully. The unique registration of the French organ is closely related to the construction of the music. Naturally, many organists today perform Bach with varying registration, but the music is unchanged. This is not the case with French music, which requires a particular registration. It is not coincidental that the first orchestration treatise and study of orchestral color was written by Berlioz. Debussy was a natural heir to that tradition.

Traditional Japanese music has always been extremely sensitive to tone quality. Up to now I have been discussing sounds as functional units, but each pitch—E, E♭, A, for example—has a different timbral spectrum and movement. The effort to perceive such minute differences characterizes both the sensitivity of Debussy and of Japanese music.

My piece for violin and orchestra entitled *Far Calls. Coming, far!*, composed in 1980, also has an original English title, which is a quotation from the last paragraph of *Finnegans Wake* by James Joyce. When thinking about this work I had the romantic idea of distance. In experience we find distances that cannot be bridged. Here the process differs from that in *A Flock Descends into the Pentagonal Garden* in that the musical core is based on a six-note scale and its inversion (Figures 16 and 17).

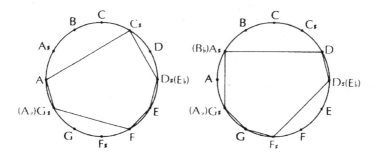

Figure 16

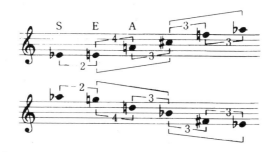

Figure 17

According to a commentary on *Finnegans Wake*, the line "Far Calls. Coming, far!" is a joyful outcry. Here "far" refers to both distance and father. I wrote this work for my daughter, so this could also mean "father is calling." The female river pouring into the male sea—a rather erotic expression. (I've always wanted to write sexy music—perhaps I should more properly say sensual music.) Not merely a male/female matter, this refers to a larger worldly sense of greater sexuality. It is about life.

To replace the image of a river flowing into the sea with a musical plan required a process similar to that used to interpret the birds' flight discussed earlier. This time the core of the music consists of a six-note motive and its inversion.

Why did I choose these pitches? I wanted to plan a tonal "sea." Here the "sea" is E♭ [*Es* in German nomenclature]-E-A, a three-note ascending motive consisting of a half step and a perfect fourth. This is extended upward from A with two major thirds and one minor third.[2] Thus, the A-major and D♭-major triads in the ascending pattern have a very bright quality when compared to the darker inversion, which, descending from A♭, had two minor triads, G-D-B♭ and B♭-G♭-E♭. Using these patterns I set the "sea of tonality" from which many pantonal chords flow. Into that sea of vibrations pours the solo violin.

In this piece there is the other key word: "far." Two perfect fifths, C-G and G♯-D♯, have a distant tonal relationship outlining the sea of tonality in low sonorities (Figure 18).

Figure 19 shows the opening measures of *Far Calls. Coming, far!*

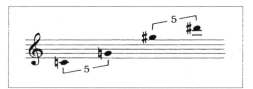

Figure 18

---

2. The author uses enharmonic equivalents in his interval description.

Figure 19. *Far Calls. Coming, Far!* © 1981 by Schott Japan, Inc.

— *II. NATURE* —

A LECTURE GIVEN ON MAY 1, 1984, AT STUDIO 200 IN TOKYO

Having discussed how I choose sounds for my music, I would like to discuss form and continuity in my compositions. Although form is very important to me, how it is realized in sound is more important. That is, construction and real sound, especially color, are inseparable in my mind. Theorists tend to think of musical form as notes on paper, as they search them for the final answer. The resultant sound is my primary concern. Rather than creating the perfect composition, I am more concerned with an approach that is closely related to my feelings and to the methods I discussed earlier.

More specifically, sound—that is, the real music in my compositions—cannot be rearranged. Most often I tend to write for an orchestra with its many instruments. In spite of the orchestra's being regarded in Western music as one gigantic instrument, I find it a source of many different sounds. The ordinary concert hall is built with the expectation that the orchestra will be blended into a single instrumental sound. I am much more interested in an orchestra that, in any given moment, can create as many different sounds as possible. For example, we can think of the orchestra as a garden, especially as a "garden for strolling," the popular Japanese landscape garden that has a variety of aspects, all in harmony without a single detail overly assertive.[3] This is the aesthetic I wish to capture in music.

In such a garden things sparkle in the sunlight, become somber when it is cloudy, change color in rain, and change form in the wind. That is the way I wish my orchestra to be. I wish to face the orchestra with my own expression, to create my own multiply focused musical garden that still reflects a greater world.

The spatial arrangement of instruments is very important to me. Even in *Dorian Horizon* (Figure 20), a piece I wrote without conscious preplanning, I was intuitively concerned about the placement of instruments. In this

---

3. Takemitsu is referring to the traditional *kaiyūshiki*, the Japanese garden he describes here.

Figure 20. *Dorian Horizon*, © 1966 by Ongaku no Tomo sha, Tokyo.

piece, written in 1964, the arrangement of the seventeen string players differs considerably from the usual seating for a string orchestra. In the front of the stage before the conductor is a string orchestra of eight players: two each of violins, violas, cellos, and basses (Figure 21). Far behind are six violins and behind those three basses (Figure 22). The greater the distance separating these groups, the better.

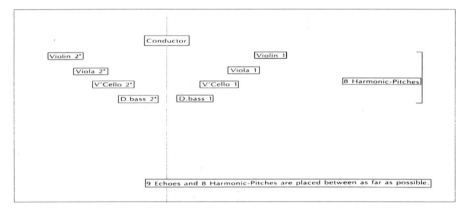

Figure 21

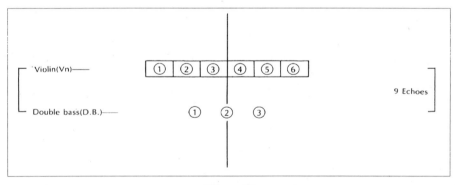

Figure 22

In this arrangement, dynamics are a crucial part of the music, since a *forte* has quite a different meaning depending on whether it is near or far. A sound, whether played *piano* or *forte*, has less meaning when heard from a distance. We perceive only the pure movement and quality of such sounds.

I have written several chamber works since *Dorian Horizon*. A piece called *Distance*, for oboe and *shō*, places the solo oboe in the front of the stage and the *shō* far behind. The oboe plays a phrase, stops, and the sound continues in the distant *shō*. The movement of sound gives a fresh experience of space.

In another of my pieces, *Garden Rain*, the brass instruments are grouped five in front, five in the rear. The work is based on a poem I found in *Miracles*, an anthology of poetry written by English-speaking children.

> "Hours are leaves of life,
> and I am their gardener....
> Each hour falls down slow."[4]

That poem by Susan Morrison, an eleven-year-old Australian girl, expresses very clearly the way I feel about music.

The work is based on a very simple mode. Recent Western music used the equal-tempered scale, but I am seriously interested in the ideal of mode. Moreover, in this instance I chose a mode with many possibilities—a mode that, beginning as a wide stream, will divide into different branches. In this mode, the perfect fifth, even if not always present in sound, is at the core of my musical perception. This interval is very important in acoustical terms, and to the human perception of sound, it could be regarded as a basic, universal module. For example, if we construct successive perfect fifths above C, we get C, G, D, A, E, B, F♯ (Figure 23, top). These open sounds are very beautiful. But if we arrange them stepwise, these pitches, with the exception of F♯, appear as the C-major scale (Figure 23, bottom). Thus, the equal-tempered scale requires the substitution of F♮. If the F♯ that appears in the cycle of perfect fifths is retained, the scale sounds unnatural.

---

4. Richard Lewis, ed. *Miracles: Poems by Children of the English-Speaking World.* Simon and Schuster, New York: 1966, p. 121.

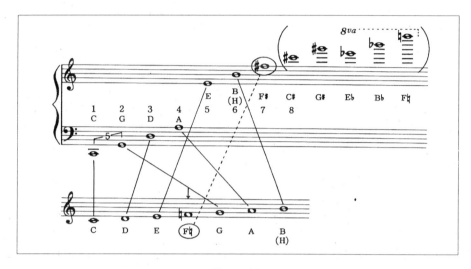

Figure 23

But I love the original, unaltered sounds and strive to use them in my music. Moreover, the stepwise arrangement of the six perfect fifths above C becomes the Lydian mode (Figure 24).

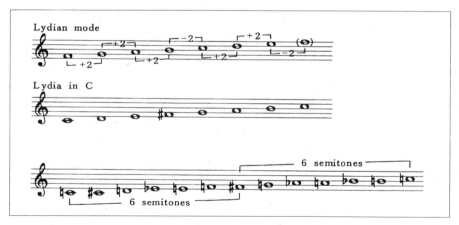

Figure 24

Interestingly, and I think rather mysteriously, my favorite pitch—F♯—appears not only in the Lydian mode but as the central point in the twelve semitones between C and its octave. To me this sound is like a mountain peak with surrounding vistas. Or, perhaps it is the main source from which C, D, and E are a lower branch stream. Furthermore, it reminds me of the eucalyptus, a primitive Australian tree that divided into many subspecies from a single root. Mode is a horizontal series of sounds, an organic series that interests me because it does not reject sounds from outside the scale.

We have learned much about modal thinking from jazz. Intuitively, musicians such as Duke Ellington and George Russell, for example, became dissatisfied with improvisations based solely on harmony. In his book *The Lydian Chromatic Concept of Tonal Organization,* published in 1959,[5] Russell studies important improvisations by Ornette Coleman and John Coltrane to arrive at a modal basis for analysis, comparing the music to the flow of the Mississippi River. With the emergence of modal thinking such as Russell's, the "blue note" began to play an important role among America's black musicians. Later, such wonderful performers as Wayne Shorter, Miles Davis, and Gil Evans grasped the intellectual basis for such music at the same time that they revived a primordial natural power that jazz had lost for a time.

Westerners, especially today, consider time as linear and continuity as a steady and unchanging state. But I think of time as circular and continuity as a constantly changing state. These are important assumptions in my concept of musical form. Sometimes my music follows the design of a particular existing garden. At times it may follow the design of an imaginary garden I have sketched. Time in my music may be said to be the duration of my walk through these gardens. I have described my selection of sounds: the modes and their variants, and the effects with shades, for example. But it is the garden that gives the ideas form (Figure 25).

---

5. George Russell. *The Lydian Chromatic Concept in Tonal Organization for Improvisation.* New York: Concepts Publishing Company, 1959.

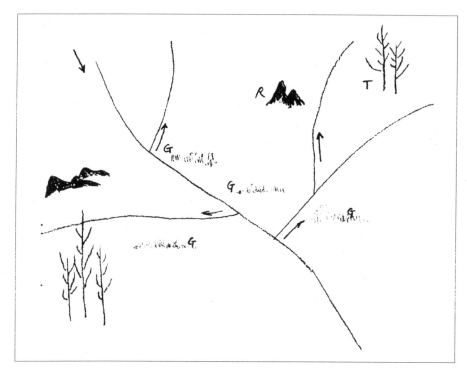

Figure 25

Imagine someone strolling through a garden such as that shown here. When writing for orchestra I often use a solo instrument—piano, cello, or violin, for example, or different groups of instruments against the orchestra. This is usually referred to as a concerto idea, but in my case it is not a concerto in the sense of a competition or contrast between soloist and orchestra.

In *Arc for Piano and Orchestra*, written in 1963 for Yūji Takahashi as soloist, the stroller is Mr. Takahashi. He has a unique way of walking that resembles limping, which is important in this piece. The work is in two sections and the direction walked in the first section is reversed in the second.

Sand and clay, the basic elements of this garden, are represented by a constant sound of strings. This constant is not used as undercoat, as in a Western painting, to emphasize other details, but exists in a way similar to the metagalaxy that surrounds our planet. Conveniently the strings are there, always sounding, representing eternity and infinity. They are the most suitable instruments to express the continuous sound of the *shō*.

Figure 26 shows the strings, which represent earth. In the garden are rocks and stones, which, in the Japanese garden, symbolize the sea or the universe. Stones may appear silent, but in relationship to their surroundings they seem to be conversing.

Figure 26. *Arc for Piano and Orchestra*, © 1976 by Editions Salabert, Paris.

In the West, too, there are ancient myths and legends in which a stone will suddenly speak about the past. In the macrocosm in which the stones exist they seem to maintain a stubborn silence but, in fact, they are quite eloquent. But compared to the others in the garden—trees or flowers, for example—they rarely move. A tree may reveal both withering and blossoming in a cycle of gradual change.

The immobile rocks and stones (indicated by *R* in my sketch [Figure 25]) are represented by low-sounding instruments. Although basically static, they undergo slight variations in shape according to the position of the stroller. Trees, grass, and flowers are individually grouped, each with a different role. Compared to the trees (*T*), the grass (*G*) undergoes greater and more rapid changes in the different cycles. Trees are represented musically by small instrumental groups.

As I mentioned, the solo piano in the middle of the score is considered the stroller (Figures 27 and 28). The pitches are precisely notated, but

Figure 27. *Arc for Piano and Orchestra*, © 1976 by Editions Salabert, Paris.

Figure 28. *Arc for Piano and Orchestra*, © 1976 by Editions Salabert, Paris.

although rhythmic proportions are controlled the tempo is up to the performer. Groups *G* and *T* move as a mobile, their relationship always unpredictable in relationship to the tempo of the piano. *G* in this work is divided into two groups: *G1* consists of flute, clarinet, contrabassoon, horn, harp, marimba, percussion, and violin. *G4* also includes flute, oboe, bass clarinet, horn, celesta, guitar, percussion, and violin. Each instrumentalist plays the assigned part in its own tempo. The performer's point of entry varies according to the pianist's cue (Figures 29 and 31).

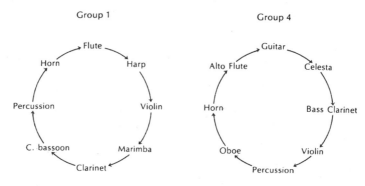

Figure 29

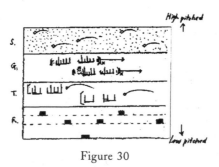

Figure 30

These varying time cycles contain what could be called heterocyclic relationships. They also show a great variety of change in quality. *T* when compared to *G* has slower, more gentle changes. Graphic notation is used for the piano and strings to make the layers of time more subtle and complex.

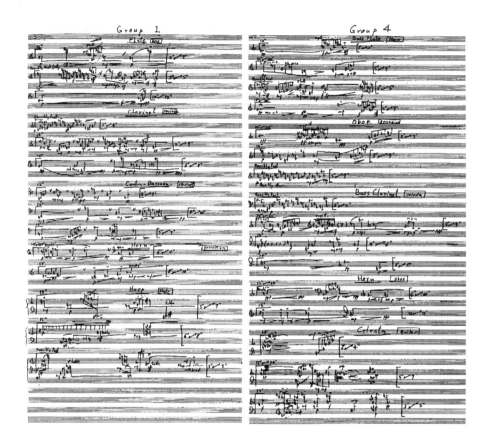

Figure 31. *Arc for Piano and Orchestra*, © 1976 by Editions Salabert, Paris.

Arc for Piano and Orchestra has several different overlapping tempi, which could be compared to scenery outside a train window. The closer scenery changes faster than the gradually changing distant views. There are the conductor's tempo, the pianist's tempo, and the tempi of individual soloists (*G* and *T*). Different times progress simultaneously; therefore this is a piece that changes shape with each performance (Figure 30).

However, in *Arc for Piano and Orchestra,* the content of the garden of music is strictly planned in advance and there are no chance elements as in a *shakkei* garden, which includes outside features.[6] Therefore, my garden is closer to those at the Katsura Detached Palace or the Saihōji Temple in Kyoto. Actually some of my works may resemble the *shakkei* in that natural sounds may be heard with the composed music. These works are close to the Shūgakuin Detached Palace.

Naturally, my music changes with how I feel physically. Compared to works from the time I wrote *Arc*, my recent pieces are much simpler. Whenever I compose, however, I sincerely wish to engage and learn from nature's precise mechanism and marvelous system. This attitude does not change. I think music must awaken natural emotion within us, an extremely sensuous process. Music is not merely notes on paper. It begins with an active listening to sound. And the ability to hear different emotions in sound is the essence of composing.

---

6. The *shakkei* is a type of Japanese garden that "borrows" existing distant scenery by including it as part of the view from its own interior.

FROM: *YUME TO KAZU* [*DREAM AND NUMBER*]. TOKYO: LIBROPORT, 1987.

Nature

People and Trees

Speaking of trees, I once heard an unforgettable story. A few days before passing away, in his failing consciousness Kenzō Nakajima told his family, "Even after dying I will be under that tree for two months." The tall tree he referred to stood in the northwest corner of his yard. Before his illness he used to tell friends, "Even without wind that fellow's leaves quiver and sing." I heard that his great joy in his last days was watching that tree from his sickbed. (When I attended his memorial service I could not see the tree from the curtained ceremonial space.)

As if following Mr. Nakajima, Shūzō Takiguchi passed away soon after. Now unattended, the kanran tree in Takiguchi's yard cast an even darker shadow. The well-developed olive tree that the poet left can best be described as gigantic. This was a sad summer. Takihiko Shibusawa suggested that those of us who admired Takiguchi should gather on July 1 every year, calling it the Kanran Memorial Day. While that may sound a little like the name of some affected literary group, I wish those memorial gatherings would continue forever.

Incidentally the error in confusing the kanran with the olive tree began in the mid-nineteenth century with the translation of the Bible into Chinese. Today the kanran instantly calls to mind an image of sunlight filtering through the dark green clusters of olives.

I hear olive trees will not grow in Tokyo. If this is true, is Takiguchi's kanran tree a miracle? What is more, that tree bore abundant olives, which so many of us shared. The poet used to bottle and label them *Rose Selavy* [*c'est la vie*]. How did that olive tree get to Japan? I don't exactly know, but I think the sculptor Toyofuku who used to live in Rome may have brought it back as a seedling.

I am fascinated by the distribution over the earth of flora, especially trees. The spread of the Australian eucalyptus, for example, is interesting. My interest all began when to my surprise I learned that a species can grow only in a limited area. Once removed from that area, beyond the seas it develops subspecies and eventually takes on a form and growth pattern different from the original. Such a history seems similar to the Diaspora of the Jews. Generally, the subject of acculturation really interests me.

In all beings there exists a single universal space that Rilke called the *Weltinnerraum* [inner-world-space]. (Perhaps it is not only trees that make us aware of that inner space.) Immobile, they show that repose with arms, palms, fingers—like Buddha.

Francis Ponge wrote, "The time of plants: they seem always fixed, immobile. Your back is turned for a few days, a week, their pose has become still more explicit, their member multiplied. Their identity allows no doubt, but their form becomes more and more realized."[1]

In a magnificent way trees transform time into space. Geometrically precise, their inner growth rings gradually expand in time to fill unlimited space. Their growth from within develops in two directions: roots below, branches and leaves above. To people branches and leaves seem trivial while roots are fundamental. In undivided action and with a glance toward infinity and eternity, leaves create chlorophyll, roots absorb minerals.

So trees exist beyond God's will and human wisdom. Yet the selfishness of humans may destroy them. And that joyful and intimate relationship of people to trees is about to be lost. No matter how sheltered the place where they grow, without asserting their presence trees concentrate self-expression, creating their own complex forms. They are trees, only trees—a passive existence without deceit. But petty human knowledge forgets this.

In a conversation with Pierre Rosteau, Le Clézio said:

> Trees have charm. They remain in the same place, immobile without self-affirmation, living a long time. In comparison humans are self-centered. When we know that humans think only of themselves and their trivial problems, while trees interfere with no one and do not steal, to us the tree stands in constant reproach, a kind of ideal.[2]

That mutually happy exchange between people and trees that once existed has become one-sided. Today we seek only to exploit them. Rilke, Redon, Emerson, Thoreau, Zeami, Bashō—as many names of people as there are trees on earth stand as testimony to that joyous exchange between people and trees.

---

1. Francis Ponge, *The Voice of Things*, ed. and trans. with an introduction by Beth Archer. New York: McGraw-Hill, 1972, p. 64.

2. Jean-Marie Gustave Le Clézio. *Conversation avec J.-M. G. Le Clézio*, ed. by Pierre Lhost. Paris: Editions Mercure de France, 1971.

Up to a certain time there was an intimacy between people and trees. A tree could develop within a human; painters and poets lived within a tree.

> One space spreads through all creatures equally—
> inner-world-space. Birds quietly flying go
> flying through us. Oh, I that want to grow,
> the tree I see outside grows in me![3]

Here is a unity of the inner and outer observed by Rilke. Such inner fulfillment of desire is about to be lost. People's sense of superiority over nature has destroyed that inner tree. How can we protect that tree— Nakajima's tree, Takiguchi's olive tree?

People and trees for people and trees. People and trees—this fleeting moment. So little time for people and trees.

---

3. Rainer Maria Rilke. *Poems 1906 to 1926*, trans. with an Introduction by J. B. Leishman. New York: New Directions, 1957, p. 193.

FROM: *ONGAKU NO YOHAKU KARA* [*FROM THE MARGIN OF THE MUSIC*]. TOKYO: SHINCHŌSHA, 1980.

Water

Late last year we moved from the center of Tokyo to Higashi Murayama City. We are supposed to have a view of Lake Tama through the southeast window of our new house, but the view is blocked by an old five-needle pine that has been designated as a monument to be preserved. The distant deep lake exists only in my imagination. The tips of the branches of that more-than-100-year-old pine shine in the sunlight as if completely covered with golden needles quivering and transmitting the deep quiet murmur of the lake.

Originally called Murayama Reservoir, Lake Tama is an artificial lake providing drinking water for Tokyo. With a turn of the faucet and through the modern maze of technology, Lake Tama pours its water into city houses. That water is already inorganic with a strong aftertaste of lime. But the source of this water now so firmly in the grip of city management still has a quiet mystery about it worthy of the name "lake." Yes, humans cannot diminish the miracle of water. What is more, we know nothing about water. We only know the temporary aspects of that shapeless entity that circulates through the universe.

About fifty years ago, when the reservoir was created, a village disappeared at the bottom of that lake. Last fall, quite unexpectedly, the lake was drained while the dam was enlarged. Television camera crews came out to show us stone hearths and the remains of homes from that lost village. My imagination was stirred when I discovered there was still a stream running in that lake bottom. But when you think about it, the sea is filled with many currents, like veins in the body. Perhaps there are many dark currents in the universe.

Why do we Japanese use the differently written but same-sounding word, *yōsui*, for amniotic fluid and for city water?

Beyond that pine tree the lake endures, as does the invisible stream within it. Enchanted by the mystery of water I wrote a piece of music using water power as the means to activate a musical instrument. The glissandi produced by water were so delicate that no other means could have reproduced that sound. Thinking of musical form I think of liquid form. I wish for musical changes to be as gradual as the tides.

Is the theory that humans evolved from water creatures credible?

I feel that water and sound are similar. The human mind conceives of water, a nonorganic substance, as if it were alive and organic. And sound, which after all consists only of physical vibrations producing soundwaves (a secret code for language!), once heard arouses various emotions in us.

We know water only in its transitory forms—rain, a lake, a river, or the sea. Music is like a river or sea. As many different currents create those oceans, so does music deepen our lives with constantly changing awareness.

FROM: *ONGAKU NO YOHAKU KARA* [*FROM THE MARGIN OF THE MUSIC*]. TOKYO: SHINCHŌSHA, 1980.

Recent Writings

In Memoriam

Music in Life

John Cage, the Elegant Revolutionary

John Cage has died. His death was unexpected.

So soon after hearing of Messiaen's death, we heard of another great loss. For me 1992 became a terrible year. For us Cage admirers this was to be the year remembered as we celebrated his eightieth birthday. That celebration had already begun in many cities in the world. What trick had fate intended?

For all, death is inevitable. In the sorrow that grips me I see not the void but the clear blue sky, and I sense the vast realm of undying death. Under no circumstance should we let sorrow close down our lives.

From Cage I learned life—or I should say, how to live and the fact that music is not removed from life. This simple, clear fact has been forgotten. Art and life have become separated, and specialists are concerned with the skeletons of methodology. Aesthetics led us to music without any relationship to live sound, mere symbols on paper.

John Cage shook the foundations of Western music and, with almost naive clarity, he evoked silence as the mother of sound. Through John Cage, sound gained its freedom. His revolution consisted of overthrowing the hierarchy in art. His ideas have been compared to Dadaism, which may not be too far off, but there are differences. His dismantling, while similar to that of Dada, is not simple negativism. For that reason his influence continues to have future possibilities.

Shortly after the war, through the intellectual antennae of Shūzō Takiguchi and Kuniharu Akiyama, I heard about Cage. But my real experience of his music came in 1961 when Ichiyanagi, on his return from a long stay in America, performed a work of Cage's in Osaka. I still feel the shock of hearing that piece. In fact, I recall that the expression "John Cage shock" originated in some comments on that music by Hidekazu Yoshida.

In those days, twelve-tone or serial music was the mainstream of the avant garde. Depending on intellectual manipulation, such music had lost a sensuality that music was originally expected to have.

The silent piece *4'33"*, premiered in 1952, has already become a legend. There are those stubborn people who do not recognize Cage as a composer of music, but only of philosophic gestures. But as we observe the works that followed, his music is no less individual than that of other composers. He is, in fact, unique.

John Cage and the Japanese have nurtured a long, intimate friendship. We can no longer see it, but as we listen to his music we recall that gentle, indescribable smile.

I know no other artist-revolutionary with the elegance of John Cage.

FROM: *TOOI YOBIGOE NO KANATA E* [*BEYOND THE FALL CALLS*]. TOKYO: SHINCHŌSHA, 1992.

The Passing of
Feldman, Nono, and Messiaen

MORTON FELDMAN, JANUARY 12, 1926–SEPTEMBER 3, 1987
LUIGI NONO, JANUARY 29, 1924–MAY 8, 1990
OLIVIER MESSIAEN, DECEMBER 10, 1908–APRIL 27, 1992

In the last few years, three composers I respected and loved have passed away, leaving me terribly sad. My feeling of loss has deepened as time passes. With the blink of time's eye they all departed on their eternal journey. No longer can we hear new works by Morton Feldman, Luigi Nono, and Olivier Messiaen.

At the time of Messiaen's death I received an interview phone call from abroad. Still in shock I blurted out, "His death leaves a crisis in contemporary music!" Days passed and I realized that spontaneous remark was not far off.

Of the three composers, the youngest departed first. We cannot discuss the fairness of life. Their deaths are our loss. Here, in these brief notes, I will share my personal recollections of these three composers.

Recently Morton Feldman's music was premiered in Japan in a program by the NHK Philharmonic's MIF (Music in Future—a title as cumbersome as Don Quixote's armor). That was the first time Feldman's orchestral music was performed in Japan. His *Coptic Light* reflects his interest in the pattern of Middle Eastern rugs, which have a regular and very fine harmony. As usual his music was quiet, the sound reminding us of pleats of soft layered light, with time standing still. And yet an indescribably rich musical space emerged. It was an exceptionally polished and elegant work in that evening's program. The concert hall was almost completely filled— unbelievable, considering that a past concert of his chamber music, entitled "Music of Today," was performed in a nearly empty hall. We were pleased that so many heard his orchestral music.

Feldman died of cancer in a Toronto hospital. Until that time he lived in Buffalo, New York. Once, delayed by a blizzard, my wife and I stayed with him for several days. Early one morning I was awakened by the sound of his piano playing. It was soft, like his music, as the vibrations were muted by the snow falling in the cold air. "Toru, come here for a minute," he called. Bending his large body over the keyboard, his face nearly touching the keys, he repeated a chord. Sensing my presence, he turned, looking at me through glasses as thick as a milk-bottle bottom, and said, "Beautiful, isn't it?" and laughed.

He was extremely nearsighted and wrote his music as if touching the notes with his eyes. Whenever I hear his music I think of its tactile quality, of his eyes "hearing" the sounds.

His music was without strong contrasts, unassertive, arising from his sensitivity—a unique minimalism without excesses. Thus the inner content of his music is clearly defined. He disliked excessive decoration. Many minimalistic pieces today drift from the cosmic to the cosmetic. With the death of Feldman will good minimalism disappear?

Considering that the last orchestral work by Luigi Nono was commissioned for Suntory Hall and that Feldman's *Coptic Light* was premiered in the same hall, I cannot escape a curious sense of Jungian synchronicity. The performance of Nono's work was also a Japanese premiere. When Nono came to Japan I learned that he was interested in the composers Feldman, Wolfgang Riehm, and Sofia Gubaidulina.

Nono was born and raised in Venice, and whenever we met he asked me to visit that city. Adored by a small group of admirers, he was called Gigi. I learned from Riehm that this nickname Gigi is written "GG." Assuming the C-major scale and solfège system, these are the syllables *sol*, *sol*, which may also mean in Italian "solitude" and "sun." Tall, with an aristocratic profile and bearing, he seemed to have a distinct aloofness about him. In reality, however, he enveloped those around him with a warmth that was like sunlight.

The piece premiered in Suntory Hall was written in memory of Andrei Tarkovskii, a Russian film director. It centered around G natural, accompanied only by microtones that echoed in space—an absolute minimalism. Why G natural? Did he anticipate his own death?

In Japan, Nono became known shortly after the war for his avant-garde style. Strict twelve-tone works seem static, without excess, like a glowing skeleton. However, he was a composer working within the tradition of Gabrieli and Monteverdi. He loved the sounds of his Venice and used to talk proudly of their influence on his music.

A copy of a score by Olivier Messiaen, which I got quite by accident from Toshi Ichiyanagi in 1950, was to have a great influence on my musical development. I am still captivated by a kind of enigmatic power in that music. But I don't intend to discuss Messiaen's music here. My spontaneous comment about the "crisis in contemporary music" brought on by Messiaen's death is beginning to clarify in my mind.

I have innumerable recollections of the man. Truly, he was my spiritual mentor. More than ten years ago, when I was to compose a piece for the same instrumentation as his *Quartet for the End of Time*, I visited Messiaen in New York. As I explained the intent of my piece to him, he related anecdotes about his own work, making many kind suggestions. When he played the piano as he discussed his instrumentation, it sounded like an orchestra. Each of his fingers seemed to make a different instrumental sound. Among the many things I learned from his music, the concept and experience of color and the form of time will be unforgettable.

The passing of these three composers—Messiaen, Nono, and Feldman—leaves a void that cannot be filled. Their music survives, reminding us of the loss of these pillars of contemporary music as we face its deepening crises.

FROM: *TOKYO MAINICHI SHINBUN* (YŪKAN), JUNE 12, 1992.

Gardener of Time

Only recently the foothills in Nagano Prefecture have begun to have the appearance of summer. Normally, even in the high altitudes here, middays are hot; but this year in mid-July there were days when the temperature did not rise above 13 or 14 degrees centigrade. There was even winterlike cold sleet. The weather bureau's satellite has been analyzing the weather, and although forecasts have been fairly accurate, still they are not dependable.

Science has been researching materials and energy. We are in an epoch of informational science, yet for us the unknown is immeasurably vast. With the knowledge that so much is beyond human control, I am somewhat relieved.

The wind begins. The mists lift. The blue-black mountains are suddenly revealed, and I look, wondering if they were always there. In such moments I feel, within, the musical impulse. This is not inspiration arising from dramatic confrontation. In nature there are subtle continuous changes as well as sudden violent changes. Perhaps I am one of those who try to see the invisible, to hear the inaudible. Human perception is not uniform but has varying levels. Therefore, what I felt cannot be experienced directly by another. But I am not alone. I live—and at the same time am made to live. By what? By whom?

My music is something like a signal sent to the unknown. Moreover, I imagine and believe that my signal meets another's signal, and the resulting physical change creates a new harmony different from the original two. And this is a continuous, changing process. Therefore, my music will not be complete in the form of a score. Rather, it refuses completion.

This is quite different from the Western artistic intention. As one who has dealt with Western music with great respect, pursuing composing as a livelihood, I have arrived at a great contradiction, which is unresolvable, and which is even enlarging.

I wonder, but cannot determine, if all Japanese (Asian, Far Eastern) composers also feel that contradiction. I am not a composer who represents Japan, not even a "Japanese" composer. Born and raised in Japan, aware that I am influenced by its culture, even as I try to free myself from that influence, at the same time I am fully aware that is impossible.

Less and less in recent times am I regarded as a "Japanese" composer (of Western music). I still experience that uncomfortable feeling when abroad. The breadth of human understanding does not seem to have widened, although there are changes. There is no doubt that the development of informational science has moved from quantity to quality and that there is a movement from regional differences toward a global culture. Though it may sound contradictory, I don't think that should be so simply done. What will simple unification produce?

There is an advantage for a Japanese composer who has studied modern Western music—music from a completely different culture. That is, he can view his own Japanese tradition from within but with another's eyes. Any culture should be understood as distinctive of an area, yet changing, free from the concept of nation or institution. Will not true mutual understanding develop only from this attitude? For the human to be independent and free seems like an infinite task. I do not stop composing, because I cannot give up hope of being one of these gardeners cultivating infinite time.

Moved by the view of those mountains, lost in thought, I found that time passed quickly and the mountains were again covered by clouds, lost from sight.

FROM: *TOKYO MAINICHI SHINBUN*, SEPTEMBER 16, 1993, P. 10.

Index

Boldface type indicates illustrations.

Permissions

Editing by Ann Basart, Thomas Finnegan, Jane Johnson, and Mimi Kusch.
Typefaces: text, Adobe Caslon; display, Truesdell; layout in PageMaker 5.0.
Scans by Peter Tannenbaum.
Jacket/cover design by Andrea Sohn.
Printed by Thomson-Shore, Michigan, on 60# Glatfelter recycled acid-free paper.